STEP · BY · STEP
VEGETABLE
COOKBOOK

EDITED BY SUSAN TOMNAY

CRESCENT BOOKS
NEW YORK

C O N T E

Sweet Spiced Baby Pumpkins, page 80.

Warm Tomato and Herb Salad, Page 108.

Red Capsicum Soup, page 66.

Vegetable Samosas, page 26.

Gourmet Vegetable Pizza, page 78.

Honeyed Baby Turnips with Lemon Thyme, page 109.

The Publisher thanks the following for their assistance in the photography for this book.
Barbara's Storehouse; Hale Imports; The Pacific East India Company; Perfect Ceramics; Villeroy & Boch; Waterford Wedgewood.

Two-cheese Risotto Cakes, page 57.

Spinach and Salmon Terrine, page 53.

Step-by-Step

When we test our recipes we rate them for ease of preparation.

A single symbol indicates a recipe that is simple and generally quick to make—perfect for beginners.

Two symbols indicate the need for just a little more care and a little more time.

Three symbols indicate special dishes that need more investment in time, care and patience—but the results are worth it.

Front cover: Sugar Peas and Carrots in Lime Butter, page 93.
Inside front cover: Herb-potato Bake (left) and Spicy Winter Casserole, page 86.
Inside back cover: Vegetable Stir-fry (top) and Pumpkin Gnocchi with Sage Butter, page 72.

Vegetable Basics

Our markets and supermarkets are overflowing with delicious and healthy vegetables. This guide to purchasing, storing, cooking and presentation will help you prepare successful and delicious vegetable dishes.

Vegetables picked fresh from the garden are still the best but, as most of us do not have a vegetable garden to harvest, we turn to the local grocery or supermarket. And there, thanks to modern methods of cold storage and transportation, we find vegetables available to us year-round that a couple of years ago were only on sale for a few short weeks. The sheer abundance and variety of vegetables, whether fresh, frozen or packaged, means that the days of meals featuring boring, boiled vegetables are banished forever.

This book brings together all the basic methods of storing, preparing and cooking vegetables to retain their color, flavor and nutrients, plus recipes from many nations. For the adventurous cook, Asian food stores and vegetable markets are full of delicious ingredients, all quite simple to prepare.

Purchasing

Little and often is a good maxim to follow when shopping for vegetables. Always buy vegetables that look fresh and crisp and have a bright natural color. Buying fresh vegetables in season is economical, and means you get the best flavor because of the short storage time.

If you have a definite vegetable recipe in mind, but can only find sad-looking specimens of the one you require, find a substitute (e.g. canned tomatoes or frozen spinach) or buy another vegetable that looks in peak condition, and save your first choice until you can find a fresh supply.

Freshness is important, especially in green leafy vegetables with a high water content, such as lettuces and spinach, because vitamin losses begin soon after picking.

Many vegetables are available ready-packed in net or plastic bags, or sometimes polystyrene trays, in convenient amounts. Before buying these, check that the produce is fresh and undamaged.

Roots and tubers – carrots, potatoes, parsnip, beets, turnips – should be unblemished, with no musty smell. Loose, unwashed potatoes are a better buy than washed and packaged ones; you can pick them over for size and quality, while the earth around the potato keeps it in good condition. Don't buy any that are sprouting or have a green tinge.

Onions, white, red or yellow, are at their sweetest when their tops are still green, but you won't find them like that in the shops, as they are picked when their tops have shriveled to allow maximum growth. Choose those with smooth skins and no dark or damp patches.

The Brassica family (all types of cabbage, Brussels sprouts, broccoli and cauliflower) should have crisp leaves; cabbages should be tightly packed and heavy; cauliflowers should be white or creamy-white, without any discolored patches. Broccoli should have firm, tight, dark green florets, not yellowed or loose-looking; avoid any that have flowered.

Buy eggplant that are firm, with shiny smooth purple skin; peppers (particularly check the red ones) and cucumbers should be crisp and quite hard, with no wrinkled skin or mushy patches – if in doubt, squeeze gently.

Tomatoes can be purchased ripe or not, according to your preference and how they are to be used. Whether you are buying large meaty types or tiny cherry tomatoes choose the reddest you can find, as firm or soft as you need (vine ripened have the best flavor,

To store mushrooms, wipe over with paper towels or a damp cloth.

Place into a brown paper bag and refrigerate for up to three days.

To store lettuce, wash, dry and loosen core by hitting on a bench or board.

Turn the lettuce over and twist out the core. Wrap and refrigerate.

Storing

Shopping frequently for vegetables means that you can take advantage of what looks best on the day, but unfortunately this is not always practical. Shopping weekly means that you must store your vegetables carefully to retain maximum flavor and vitamins.

Most vegetables benefit from being stored in a cool, dark place. Generally, vegetables keep best when stored in the crisper section of the refrigerator. Store them unwashed and loosely packed in plastic bags. Squeeze the air out of the bags before storing. Fresh ginger can be refrigerated unwrapped.

Leafy green vegetables such as lettuce and spinach should be washed and thoroughly dried by spinning or patting dry with a dish towel or paper towels. (Water washes out vitamins from the leaves.) Hit the base of the lettuce hard on the counter or sink to loosen the core, then turn over and twist it out. Pack whole lettuce or leaves loosely in plastic bags. Squeeze air out of the bag, seal and place in the crisper section of the refrigerator. Properly stored, lettuces will last up to seven days for iceberg and two to three days for soft butter types.

although they may be hard to find). Leave firm tomatoes to ripen at room temperature. Keep in mind that canned tomatoes are perfect for many dishes.

Legumes (green beans, fava beans, etc, and peas, sugar snap peas and snow peas) should be bright green and have no wrinkles in the skin. Smaller specimens are younger and therefore more tender. They should 'snap' rather than bend when broken.

Sweet corn is also best when young. This summer treat should be delicious enough to eat raw, but usually has become a little too tough by the time it reaches the shelf. Choose cobs with unblemished husks. Pull the husks back to check that the kernels are even-sized, small and tender, and that there are no caterpillars lurking. Dented-looking kernels mean the corn is not fresh and will be tough when cooked.

Freshness is particularly important with salad vegetables. Don't buy green vegetables that are wilted, dry-looking or have yellow or brown patches or insect-nibbled leaves. Crisp-head lettuces (iceberg, romaine) should feel firm when squeezed and the base should be dry. Many loose-head lettuces are sold with their roots

intact; this helps to keep them in good condition.

Stalky vegetables, such as celery, fennel and asparagus, should be crisp and firm with no brown patches. Celery should be heavy and stand up straight, with light green leaves. Fennel should be white and crunchy.

When buying asparagus, choose straight even-sized stalks with tight buds – thick stalks are more tender than thin. The cut end should be dry but not withered.

Artichokes should have silky, compact green heads with no dark patches.

Choose avocados according to what you are using them for. For example, you may want a really ripe one to puree, a perfect one to eat immediately or a firmer one to keep. Press gently to test for ripeness; the flesh should just give at the stem end. Avoid those with bruised or black/brown patches. Place hard avocados in a brown paper bag and put the bag in a warm place (e.g. on top of the refrigerator, at the back over the motor) to ripen in two days.

Bunches of fresh green herbs such as parsley, chives and basil are best kept in water in the shop, and should look and smell freshly picked.

Mushrooms can be stored in the refrigerator, but should be wiped clean and placed in a brown paper bag. This way they will keep in good condition for three to four days. Do not store them in plastic because they will begin to decay quickly.

Potatoes should not be refrigerated as they can develop a sweetish taste. To store, remove from plastic bags and place in a cloth or paper bag. Keep them in a cool, dark, dry place with good ventilation. Properly stored, they should remain in good condition for two months or more. Sweet potatoes, turnips, onions (except for scallions) and garlic should be stored in the same manner.

For convenience, both raw garlic and ginger can be pureed in a food processor or blender and stored in glass jars in the refrigerator.

Tomatoes are a sub-tropical crop and low temperatures damage their cell structure, so they should not be refrigerated. The optimum storage temperature for tomatoes is about 20°F, but keeping them at room temperature until needed is best for

To prepare asparagus, break off the hard ends and discard.

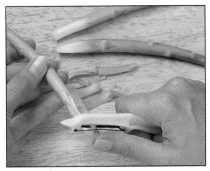

Trim any remaining woody ends with a vegetable peeler.

most cooks, and underripe fruit will ripen best at room temperature. Take tomatoes out of plastic bags to avoid the growth of bacteria. Keep them away from sunlight – it destroys vitamin C. Store in a single layer unless you want the tomatoes to ripen quickly, as heat rather than light causes ripening. Remove any tomatoes that have spoiled.

Freezing

Most fresh vegetables are not suitable to freeze raw, but many can be blanched, then successfully frozen. Blanched asparagus spears, beans, broccoli, carrots, cauliflower, corn (whole ears or kernels), shelled peas and skinned tomatoes all freeze well. Freezing is a good way to take advantage of a seasonal glut in produce.

Pick over and discard any damaged specimens. Wash and cut the vegetable into pieces as desired. Plunge into boiling water for 30 seconds, then into ice water to refresh. Pat dry with paper towels, pack into freezer bags, expel air and seal. Label and freeze. Frozen blanched vegetables will keep for up to three months.

Fresh herbs can be successfully frozen. Wash and dry the leaves, place into small freezer bags, expel air and seal. Label and freeze.

To freeze cooked vegetables dishes, stock, purees, soups and sauces, cool the just-cooked dish quickly, place in plastic containers, seal, label and freeze. As a general rule, freeze for up to two months.

Commercial or home-frozen vegetables should be added to recipes unthawed, and toward the end of the cooking time.

Stocks, sauces and precooked dishes should be thawed in the refrigerator and reheated gently before serving.

To salt eggplant, place the chopped vegetable in colander, sprinkle over salt.

Preparing

Before cooking, wash vegetables well to remove any pesticide residue as well as grit or insects. Leeks, spinach and Swiss chard all need to be washed thoroughly to remove sand.

Some vegetables require particular techniques to cook and present them at their best. The following methods are frequently used in this book.

Salting is used when cooking eggplant and large zucchini or cucumbers, to draw out excess moisture and any bitterness from the vegetable. Salting eggplant slices before frying will cut the amount of oil needed by two-thirds. To salt vegetables, chop or slice according to the recipe. Place in a large colander or spread on paper towels and sprinkle with salt. Leave for at least 30 minutes, rinse under cold water, drain and pat dry with paper towels.

To peel tomatoes, make a small cross on the bottom of each tomato, and plunge into boiling water for 30 seconds. Lift out and plunge into chilled water for one minute, using plenty of water in each case. The skin can then be peeled easily from the cross using a downward motion.

To prepare artichokes, trim the

After 30 minutes, rinse under cold water and pat dry with paper towels.

stalk from base of artichoke. Using scissors, trim hard points from the outer leaves. Using a sharp knife, cut top from artichoke. Brush all cut areas with lemon juice to prevent discoloration. Cook artichokes in a stainless steel or enamel pan.

To prepare asparagus, break off the inedible woody ends and discard. If the ends are still hard, trim with a vegetable peeler.

To prepare avocado, cut the avocado in half using a sharp knife. To remove the pit, push the knife into the pit and gently twist and lift out. The skin can be peeled off with fingers.

To prepare cucumber, when seeding is called for in the recipe, peel the cucumber using a vegetable peeler (if peeling is specified), halve lengthwise and scrape out the seeds with a teaspoon and discard. Cucumbers can be given a decorative finish by peeling in stripes, or by running the tines of a fork down the outside after peeling. Use as directed.

To crush garlic cloves, peel the garlic and place on a cutting board. Using a very sharp knife, chop the garlic finely, working in a little salt as you go. Scrape the chopped garlic together into a mound. Turn it over

To peel, make a cross cut in each tomato and plunge into hot water.

Plunge into cold water, then peel skin down from the cut.

To chop onions, make five or six cuts through, turn and slice across.

To prepare artichokes, cut off ends with a sharp knife.

Trim leaves with scissors and brush cut ends with lemon juice.

To remove avocado pits, place knife blade firmly into pit.

Gently twist the knife and lift out the pit.

with the blade, chop again. Repeat until garlic is a fine mass. For coarsely crushed garlic, press down heavily with the flat of a wide knife or cleaver.

Cutting the garlic clove lengthwise makes it easier to remove the skin.

To prepare mushrooms. Never peel or wash mushrooms. After wiping clean, remove stems if they are woody (reserve to make stock) and slice. Peeling and washing mushrooms removes flavor and makes them waterlogged.

To prepare onions. Peel and place on a chopping board. To chop, make five or six slices through the onion. Turn it 90°, hold layers together firmly and cut across them.

Cooking methods

Vegetables can be cooked in many ways, ranging from burying them in the ashes of a campfire to combining with eggs and liqueur to make a most sophisticated soufflé.

The three cooking methods that have a particular significance for vegetables are blanching, steaming and stir-frying. These are all quick-cooking and retain all the color, flavor and nutrition of the vegetables.

Blanching. This method is used to precook (or parboil) vegetables before adding to other cooked dishes or salads, or before freezing. The vegetables are plunged briefly into boiling water and then refreshed in cold water. This method preserves the green color.

Steaming. Vegetables are cut into even-sized pieces and cooked in a basket or on a rack over a little boiling water or stock in a tightly covered pan. A few minutes steaming (depending on size) is enough to make green vegetables tender while remaining firm and flavorful (root vegetables take longer). This method is preferable to boiling because the flavor is preserved as the vegetable juices are not lost in the cooking water.

Stir-frying. Heat a little oil in a large frying pan or wok. Have all the vegetables cut or divided into thin even-sized pieces. Cutting celery, carrots, etc, on the diagonal gives a larger surface area and enables quicker cooking than straight sliced vegetables. When the oil is hot, add the vegetables. Toss and stir briskly around the pan for a few minutes, using a large spatula (not plastic) or spoon, over high heat. Do not let the vegetables sit still in the pan, or they will burn.

Never soak vegetables in water prior to cooking or add soda to the cooking water, as both these methods destroy vitamin C.

Vegetable Juices

A quick and healthy way to make the most of vegetables is to extract the juice from them. Vegetable drinks, alone or combined with other vegetable and fruit juices make an ideal vitamin-packed pick-me-up, instant breakfast, or can be used to add extra vitamins and minerals to your diet.

Wash or peel vegetables and cut into chunks that will fit into your juice extractor. To minimize vitamin loss, cut vegetables immediately before juicing and drink the juice as soon as it is made.

Vegetables suitable for juicing are carrots, celery, tomatoes, parsley, cucumber, peppers, cabbage, beets and onion. Carrot juice has a smooth and velvety texture and soothes a troubled stomach; cabbage and onion juices are reputed to help those suffering from colds; parsley, cucumber and celery juice purify the blood, while cucumber is also said to help remove cellulite.

Try these delicious juice combinations: carrot and apple; carrot, celery and apple; tomato and celery; tomato, onion and parsley; carrot, beet and celery.

Canned tomato juice makes the basis for an instant gazpacho: place chopped pepper, chopped tomato, chopped cucumber, chopped celery, a little chopped onion, a crushed garlic clove and chopped parsley in food processor or blender, process until almost smooth. Stir in chilled canned tomato juice to the correct consistency. Season to taste with salt, freshly ground black pepper and a little lemon juice and serve. Store, covered, in refrigerator.

ARTICHOKE: Although there are two types of artichoke – globe (pictured fresh and canned), and Jerusalem, the globe is the most often seen. Simply trim off outer leaves, steam for 30 minutes, then peel off the leaves one by one and dip them in melted butter, vinaigrette or hollandaise. The Jerusalem artichoke is a root vegetable from the sunflower family, which can be included in stews and soups, pureed, steamed or fried, or eaten raw in salads.

ASPARAGUS: Held in high esteem in Europe, the white type is not as popular in America where the peak season for bright green asparagus is in the spring. A very light and delicate vegetable, asparagus lends itself well to rich sauces, such as hollandaise. It can also be served cold in salads, or on its own with a simple vinaigrette or mustard dressing.

AVOCADOS: The avocado was first introduced in restaurants, crowned with fresh shrimp and cocktail sauce, or served simply with vinaigrette dressing. It has long since proved its versatility, chopped and tossed in salads, sliced on sandwiches, or mashed with garlic and lemon to make a guacamole dip. It is actually a fruit, and in parts of South-east Asia is eaten with sugar as a dessert.

BASIL: This herb has a uniquely strong flavor and scent. It is traditionally and extensively used in Italian cooking in tomato-based sauces and as the main ingredient in pesto. Add whole or chopped leaves to salads, soups and pasta dishes.

BEANS: Despite the wide variety in the bean family – French, string, purple (which turn green when cooked), yellow wax, snake – the green bean (pictured) is the most popular. Beans may be topped and tailed and strings removed, sliced thinly with a bean slicer or cut diagonally into short lengths. Use in casseroles and stir-fries, or blanch for use in salads.

BEETS: A hardy root vegetable, the beet is celebrated in the Russian soup, borscht. It also lends itself to pickling in vinegar, spices and brown sugar and is used in salads. Baby beets can be served whole as a vegetable topped with sour cream. Raw beets have a pleasant nutty taste; the leaves can be cooked in the same way as spinach.

BROCCOLI: A cousin of the cauliflower, broccoli can be white, purple or green, the latter most commonly found in Western cuisine. It can be lightly steamed and eaten plain or with a sauce as a side dish, and incorporated in casseroles and stir-fries. Sprouting vegetables such as broccoli and cauliflower should never be overcooked.

CABBAGE: As well as the more common red and green cabbages shown, the loose-headed savoy is worth trying. Cabbage should be steamed or lightly pan-fried, rather than boiled, and should retain some crispness when cooked. To keep its color, red cabbage needs to be cooked with an acidic ingredient such as apple or wine. Raw cabbage is used to make coleslaw.

CARROTS: Sweet, crunchy carrots must be one of the most popular vegetables, particularly with children. A root vegetable, they can be served steamed, caramelized, and as a side dish, used in all manner of cooked dishes, or cut into matchstick strips as a salad ingredient or as part of a platter of crudités. Baby or Dutch carrots can simply be washed and eaten whole, cooked or raw. Leave the leafy top intact and serve with a dip at parties or add to school lunchboxes. Carrots are loaded with vitamin A and fiber.

CAULIFLOWER: A vegetable with a long history, first introduced into Europe in the 13th century, the cauliflower consists of a head of tightly packed pretty white florets encased in tough leaves. The florets are an attractive addition to salads (use them blanched or raw) or stir-fried dishes. Cauliflower should be cooked only until tender to retain vitamins and flavor. It is popularly served with a creamy cheese sauce. Baby cauliflowers can be served whole, one per person.

CELERY: Most often eaten raw as a salad vegetable, sometimes in decorative curls, celery is frequently used in Italian cookery and in poultry and pork stuffing. It is delicious braised and served as a side dish, with a white sauce. Use the leafy top as a flavoring for cooked dishes.

CHILI: From the pepper family, chilies are spicy and very highly flavored. The smaller and redder the chili the hotter it is (such as the tiny bird's eye, pictured here). Chili is used as a spice more than as a vegetable and is rarely ever eaten whole. Finely sliced or crushed into a paste it is added to Mexican, Indian and Asian

food. Use chilies with caution until you decide how much heat you like in a particular dish. To reduce heat, cut off the membranes and seeds and discard.

CHINESE VEGETABLES: Pictured are some of the many varieties readily available in Chinese grocery stores and supermarkets. Bok choy is a type of cabbage (this variety is short with white stems). Choy sum resembles spinach and has yellow flowers. Leafy vegetables add color and warmth to braised dishes and combine well also with meats, noodles and oyster, mushroom and black bean sauces. These vegetables are blanched and added to noodle soups at the last minute, finely chopped as a garnish or served as a side dish. Long snake beans (doh gok) are included in many South-east Asian stir-fries, curries and soups.

CHIVES: This mild herb is a member of the onion and garlic family. Its subtle taste combines well and the small green flecks of chopped chives are attractive against the pale colors of scrambled eggs, mashed potato and white sauces. The pretty blue flowers are edible and can be used in salads.

CILANTRO: A leafy green plant with tubular roots, this herb adds a crisp, spicy freshness and full flavor to Thai, Indian and Mexican food (with some disliking its strong, earthy flavor). Use the leaves in salads and salsa. The roots may be ground and added to curry paste.

CORN: Originally from South America, this vegetable is available both fresh and packaged. Corn on the cob and baby corn are fresh and plentiful in summer; when not available, use canned creamed corn or canned or frozen corn niblets. Corn is versatile; use it in fritters, in soup, chowder, or Asian dishes. Barbecue or steam whole cobs and serve hot with butter, salt and pepper.

CUCUMBER: Popular around the world for its cooling properties, fresh cucumber is combined with yogurt in India to accompany curries, mixed with yogurt and garlic in Greece as a dip, peeled and used in sandwiches in England, added to gazpacho (cold soup) in Spain. The smaller variety are crisper and have a better flavor than larger table ones. Apple cucumbers are white, spherical and are excellent in salads.

DILL: A sweet-scented herb of the parsley family, with soft thin feathery leaves, dill is often used as a garnish for fish such as fresh salmon or trout, and goes well with egg dishes and sauces. It is used for pickling (hence dill pickles) and to make dill vinegar. Dill seeds, which have a stronger flavor than the leaves, are also available.

EGGPLANT: Also known as aubergine, eggplant is available all year round, and comes in a number of shapes ranging from globe, egg and sausage, and colors from white through to the more usual purple. It originated in India, and was quickly adopted by the Arabs. Today it is found in many cuisines. The classic dish made with eggplant is the Greek moussaka, and it is also used in Indian curries, or stuffed or baked on its own. Cold grilled eggplant is also found in salads and on antipasto platters, and in Italian-style foccacia sandwiches. Baby eggplant may be pickled in vinegar with garlic and oregano and used like pickled gherkins.

FENNEL: A squat, bulbous plant which looks like a celery heart, fennel has soft feathery leaves similar to those of dill. It has an anise flavor, and looks and tastes particularly good in stews, especially those using fish, pork or veal. The fennel plant grows in abundance in the Mediterranean region, and is thus used widely in Italian and other food of the area. Fennel can also be sliced into thin strips and used raw in salads, or cut in half lengthwise, steamed and served with cheese sauce.

GARLIC: Although there are several different types – red-skinned, violet and the large elephant garlic, the white garlic is the one most often seen. Used with discretion, it adds delicious flavor to cooked dishes, and raw it enhances salad dressings. If a milder flavor is preferred, whole cloves can be browned, then removed before the rest of the cooking.

GINGER: One of the oldest and most commonly used spices, particularly in Asian cooking, ginger comes in two forms. Raw or 'green' ginger is the root in its natural form; it is peeled and chopped to flavor stir-fries and curries. Fresh chopped green ginger is available in jars. Dried, ground ginger is mainly used in baking.

LETTUCE: No longer is lettuce synonymous with the traditional iceberg variety (lower left). Pictured are just some of those available (clockwise from top left): red leaf, romaine, the unusual red coral, and salad mix (mesclun).

Lettuces fall into two general types – those with a firm, tightly packed head, and loose leaf lettuce, with no heart. The former are perfect used as cups for salads and Asian stir-fry dishes, while the latter can be picked a few leaves at a time as needed. Salad mix is a combination of a variety of baby lettuce leaves and edible flowers. A simple vinaigrette dressing will turn a bowl of mixed lettuce leaves into a special salad, but lettuce also lends itself to brief cooking, and makes a delicious soup.

MUSHROOMS: The common cultivated mushroom can be bought at three stages: (from top) the tiny buttons, slightly large cap mushrooms, which can be stuffed, and the larger flat (or field) mushrooms, which have more flavor than the smaller ones. Oyster mushrooms (at bottom) are also cultivated. They are chewier than the common variety, and have a shellfish flavor. **Note:** Do not be tempted by wild mushrooms; some varieties are highly poisonous.

ONIONS: Invaluable as a seasoning in most cuisines, onions also stand in their own right as a vegetable. Yellow onions (left) have the strongest flavor; they are excellent in soups and stews. White onions (center) are milder, often served raw in salads and used for stir-fries or else caramelized until golden-brown. Mostly eaten raw, red or Italian onions (right) are from a different family, and have a mild nutty taste.

PARSLEY, CURLY: Chopped or in whole sprigs, this biennial herb usually makes its appearance as a garnish. It is also used in soups, stews and pasta dishes, marrying particularly well with carrots, celery, cabbage, cauliflower, eggplant and spinach, and providing a rich source of vitamins, especially A and D, and minerals.

PARSLEY, FLAT-LEAF: Also known as continental parsley, flat-leaf parsley is used interchangeably with curly parsley, depending on preference. It does not keep quite as long as its cousin, but some prefer its stronger flavor and claim it has a less bitter taste.

PARSNIPS: Enjoyed by many who glaze parsnips with brown sugar and fruit juice, this vegetable is a close relative of the carrot, but sweeter. It is served baked with a roast dinner, pureed, and is also used in soups (add a chopped parsnip to pea and ham soup) and in casseroles.

PEAS: Members of the large legume family, peas appear in many different guises. Pictured are (from top) the sweet-flavored snow peas and sugar snap peas (both are good eaten whole), frozen peas, split peas and fresh garden peas. Snow peas are also called mange tout, meaning 'eat everything', but in fact you may like to nip off the top and pull the string down the side. Frozen peas serve a useful purpose for quick and easy cooking, but do not have the flavor of fresh garden peas, especially young ones. Try to shell fresh green peas just before they are cooked, so that they do not dry out. Dried, split peas are used for soup and purees, and can substitute for lentils in some recipes. They require long, slow cooking, but should not need soaking.

PEPPERS: Peppers are readily available in red and green forms, sometimes yellow, and occasionally in a dark purple that is almost black. In Britain they are known as sweet peppers, as indeed they are. Delicious raw, they can be cut into rounds or neat strips and used for dressing up salads. Cooked, they add a distinctive flavor to tomato-based casseroles. Whole peppers can be stuffed with a meat or rice mixture and baked; red peppers are superb grilled, peeled and used in salads, savory tarts or antipasto platters.

POTATOES: Although there are literally hundreds of varieties of potato grown throughout the world, you will commonly find only three or four at the grocers. Russet or Idaho potatoes (left) are floury and best for mashing. They can also be baked successfully, as can the red potato. The red holds its shape well, and is good for sliced potato bakes. New potatoes (top right) can be boiled and used in potato salad, and baby ones just need steaming.

PUMPKIN (SQUASH): In the United States, the different varieties of pumpkin are known as winter squash to distinguish them from the soft-skinned summer squashes. They are all part of the gourd family. Buttercup squash (top), has pale yellow meat and a sweet flavor. But for a pleasant change, try the butternut or little golden nuggets. As well as baking, squash are pureed, made into soup and used in pumpkin pie.

ROSEMARY: An herb with a pungent aroma somewhat like pine needles, rosemary should be used with care, lest it overpower the other ingredients. It is excellent with lamb and some mild-flavored vegetables such as cabbage, squash and zucchini, and is one of the ingredients of a bouquet garni. Bunches of fresh rosemary can easily be hung up to dry and stored in an airtight container for future use.

SCALLIONS: Members of the onion family, both the slender scallion and bulbous green onion (pictured at top) contribute a delicate flavor to many dishes. Leeks (middle)

stand as a vegetable on their own, as well as being used in soups, quiches and savory tarts. Small shallots (bottom), similar in shape to garlic, have reddish-brown skin and purple-tinged white flesh and a mild flavor.

SPEARMINT: We call it mint, but the long-pointed leafed herb we most commonly use is spearmint, just one of the members of the mint family. Probably its best-known use is for mint sauce to accompany lamb,

but it is also an important ingredient in Thai cooking, and adds flavor to boiled peas and potatoes. Mint leaves dry well in the microwave oven, keeping their color and scent.

SPINACH: Although the two leafy greens pictured are both frequently described as spinach, they are from two different families. The large, textured leaves are *Beta vulgaris*, also

known as Swiss chard. At left is the true spinach, the small, flat-leafed *Spinacea oleracea*, also known as English spinach. This has a much milder flavor, and as well as being cooked in many well-known dishes, makes an excellent salad.

SWEET POTATO: No relation to the potato, the sweet potato is similar in that it is also a tuber. The three varieties shown differ mainly in their coloring (from left: red, white and orange). The sweet potato is also sometimes known as yam in some countries. All are cooked in the same ways as potatoes, although sugar is sometimes used to emphasize their natural sweetness.

TOMATOES: Technically a fruit rather than a vegetable, tomatoes are, however, used exclusively in savory dishes. Vine and roma (or plum) tomatoes are used interchangeably for cooking and salads – they are indispensable in Mediterranean cuisine. Little cherry tomatoes and the relatively new yellow pear variety are most commonly eaten raw, although they may be quickly stir-fried. The fashionable sundried tomatoes (at bottom) may be rehydrated and used in

place of fresh, but are more often found raw in salads and sandwiches. Bought tomatoes may need ripening for some days to develop full flavor.

TURNIPS: Like potatoes, turnips are a root vegetable, with variety in shape and color, but all with a similar peppery taste. Baby turnips are relative newcomers to our fruit markets. They only need to be washed, topped and tailed to be used whole in dishes such as navarin of lamb or used raw in salads. Turnip tops may be washed and cooked in the same way as spinach.

ZUCCHINI: In America, zucchini and the little yellow and green squash shown are all known generically as summer squash, while zucchini are actually baby marrows. Young and tender, they need only to be steamed briefly and served with butter and a little black pepper. Zucchini combine well with tomatoes, and are used in ratatouille. The flowers can also be stuffed with a savory mixture, then dipped in batter and deep-fried in oil.

SNACKS

CHEESE AND OLIVE SQUARES

Preparation time: 15 minutes
Total cooking time: 15 minutes
Makes about 20 pieces

1 medium red onion
1/4 cup pitted black olives
1 medium red pepper
1 medium green pepper
2 tablespoons fresh basil
   leaves
3 teaspoons balsamic vinegar
2 cloves garlic, crushed
1/4 cup oil
3 cloves garlic, crushed,
   extra
1 large (12 x 16 inch) piece of
   focaccia
4 oz cheddar cheese,
   grated
fresh basil leaves or other fresh
   herbs to garnish

➤ PREHEAT OVEN to moderate 350°F. Line a baking sheet with foil.
1 Slice onion and olives. Cut peppers in halves. Remove seeds and membrane. Cut into fine strips. Finely shred basil leaves.
2 Combine peppers, onion, olives, basil, vinegar and garlic in a medium bowl. Mix well. Cover and set aside.
3 Combine oil and extra garlic in a small bowl. Using a serrated knife, slice focaccia horizontally through center. Brush focaccia halves with combined oil and garlic. Arrange the combined olive and pepper filling evenly over the bottom half of focaccia. Sprinkle with cheese and top with remaining focaccia piece. Place on the prepared baking sheet. Bake 15 minutes or until the cheese melts. Cut into squares, garnish with basil leaves and serve hot or at room temperature.

COOK'S FILE

Storage time: Olive and pepper filling can be made one day in advance. Store, covered, in the refrigerator. Assemble and cook squares just before serving.
Hints: Focaccia is flat Italian bread, available from most delicatessens, bakeries and some grocers.
To crush garlic, peel cloves and lay on cutting board. Place the flat side of a large chef's knife over the garlic and push down hard with the flat of your hand. Chop finely.
Variations: If focaccia is unavailable, use small bread rolls sliced in half, slices of large round loaves or sliced baguette.
Any of these ingredients can be added to the filling: Sliced fresh mushrooms, marinated mushrooms, grilled eggplant slices, marinated artichoke hearts, drained and sliced, sliced salami, ham or prosciutto (Parma ham), sliced turkey or chicken breast, small fresh peeled shrimp or sundried tomatoes.

PHYLLO VEGETABLE POUCHES

Preparation time: 45 minutes
Total cooking time: 35–40 minutes
Makes 12

8 sheets phyllo pastry
1/2 cup butter, melted
1/2 cup sesame seeds

Filling
3 cups grated carrot
2 large onions, finely
    chopped
1 tablespoon grated ginger
1 tablespoon finely chopped
    fresh cilantro
1 cup water

8 oz can water chestnuts, rinsed
    and sliced
1 tablespoon miso
1/4 cup tahini paste
pepper to taste

➤ PREHEAT OVEN to moderate 350°F. Brush two baking pans with melted butter or oil.

1 **To make Filling:** Combine carrot, onions, ginger, cilantro and water in large pan. Cover, cook over low heat 20 minutes. Uncover, cook a further 5 minutes or until all liquid has evaporated. Remove from heat, cool slightly. Stir in water chestnuts, miso and tahini. Season with pepper.

2 Place one sheet of phyllo pastry on work surface. Brush lightly with butter. Top with another three pastry

sheets, brushing between each layer. Cut phyllo into six even squares. Repeat process with remaining pastry giving 12 squares in total.

3 Divide filling evenly between each square, placing filling in the center. Bring edges together and pinch to form a pouch. Brush the lower portion of each pouch with butter; press in sesame seeds. Place on prepared pans. Bake 10–12 minutes or until golden brown and crisp. Serve hot with sweet chili sauce, if desired.

COOK'S FILE

Storage time: Cook just before serving. Assemble pouches up to one day in advance. Store in refrigerator.
Hint: Miso is a salty soy bean paste, available from Asian food stores.

1

2

3

SPINACH CROQUETTES WITH MINTED YOGURT SAUCE

Preparation time: 50 minutes
Total cooking time: 25 minutes +
  1 hour refrigeration
Makes 18

1¹/2 cups short-grain rice
8 oz feta cheese, crumbled
¹/4 cup grated Parmesan cheese
2 eggs, lightly beaten
1 clove garlic, crushed
2 teaspoons grated lemon rind
¹/2 cup chopped scallions
9 oz packet frozen chopped
  spinach, drained, squeezed of
  excess moisture
1 tablespoon freshly chopped
  dill
2 cups fine dry bread crumbs
2 eggs, lightly beaten, extra
oil for deep frying

Yogurt sauce
8 oz plain yogurt
2 tablespoons chopped mint
2 tablespoons lemon juice
salt and freshly ground black
  pepper to taste

➤ COOK RICE in a large pan of boiling water until just tender; drain, rinse under cold water, drain again.

1 Combine rice, cheeses, eggs, garlic, lemon, scallions, spinach and dill in a large bowl. Using wet hands, divide the mixture into 18 portions. Roll each portion into even-sized sausage shapes. Place on tray. Refrigerate for 30 minutes.

2 Spread bread crumbs on a sheet of wax paper. Dip croquettes into extra beaten egg mixture. Coat with bread crumbs; shake off excess. Refrigerate a further 30 minutes.

3 To make Yogurt Sauce: Combine yogurt, mint, lemon juice, salt and pepper in a bowl. Mix well. Cover, refrigerate until needed.

4 Heat oil in a deep heavy-based pan. Gently lower batches of croquettes into moderately hot oil with tongs or slotted spoon. Cook over medium high heat 2–3 minutes or until golden and crisp and cooked through. Drain on paper towel. Repeat with remaining croquettes. Serve croquettes hot or cold with Yogurt Sauce.

COOK'S FILE

Storage time: Croquettes can be made up to two days in advance. Cook just before serving.

Variation: Use fresh and lightly steamed spinach in place of frozen spinach if preferred. Use the same amounts.

CAULIFLOWER FRITTERS WITH TOMATO RELISH

Preparation time: 35 minutes
Total cooking time: 30 minutes
Serves 4–6

1 small cauliflower
¾ cup all-purpose flour
1 teaspoon ground cumin
½ teaspoon baking
    soda
⅔ cup water
1 egg
6½ oz plain yogurt
vegetable oil for deep
    frying

Tomato Relish
2 tablespoons vegetable oil
1 medium onion, finely
    chopped
14½ oz can diced tomatoes
½ cup white wine vinegar
¾ cup sugar
1 clove garlic, crushed
1 teaspoon ground cumin
½ cup golden raisins
¾ cup finely chopped fresh
    cilantro

➤ CUT CAULIFLOWER into large florets. Remove as much of the stem as possible without breaking florets. Wash and drain well. Pat dry with paper towels.

1 Combine flour, cumin and baking soda in a medium mixing bowl. Make a well in the center. Beat together water, egg and yogurt. Add to dry ingredients. Using a wooden spoon, stir until batter is smooth and free of lumps. Leave for 10 minutes.

2 To make Tomato Relish: Place the oil, onion, tomatoes, vinegar, sugar, garlic, cumin and raisins in a medium pan. Cover, cook over medium heat for 10 minutes. Bring to a boil, reduce heat and simmer, uncovered, 5 minutes or until mixture thickens and darkens slightly. Remove from heat. Stir in cilantro.

3 Heat oil in deep heavy-based pan. Dip florets in batter, drain off excess. Using a metal spoon or tongs, gently lower cauliflower into hot oil in small batches. Cook until golden brown, 3–5 minutes. Lift out with a slotted spoon and drain on paper towels. Serve hot with the Tomato Relish.

COOK'S FILE

Storage time: The Tomato Relish can be prepared up to three days in advance and stored, covered, in the refrigerator.
The batter can also be prepared up to three days in advance and stored, covered, in the refrigerator until required. However, if you do this, make sure to remove the batter from the refrigerator about two hours before it is needed and bring it to room temperature before dipping the florets.

1

2

3

THAI CORN PANCAKES WITH CILANTRO MAYONNAISE

Preparation time: 15 minutes
Total cooking time: 5 minutes each
batch
Serves 6

2 cloves garlic
1 small red chili
3/4 inch piece fresh ginger
15 1/4 oz can sweet corn kernels,
    drained
2 eggs
1/4 cup cornstarch
2 tablespoons fresh cilantro
    leaves
freshly ground black pepper
1 tablespoon sweet chili sauce
1 tablespoon peanut oil

Cilantro Mayonnaise
2/3 cup whole egg mayonnaise
1/4 cup lime juice
**1/3 cup cilantro leaves,
    chopped**
8 scallions, finely chopped
**freshly ground black pepper
    to taste**

➤ ROUGHLY CHOP garlic; chop chili and ginger.

1 Place half the sweet corn, eggs, cornstarch, cilantro, garlic, chili, ginger, pepper and chili sauce in food processor bowl. Using the pulse action, process 30 seconds or until mixture is smooth. Transfer mixture to medium bowl and fold in the remaining corn.

2 Heat oil in a large frying pan. Spoon two tablespoons of corn mixture into pan and cook over a medium heat for 2–3 minutes or until golden. Turn over and cook the second side for 1–2 minutes or until cooked through. Repeat process until all mixture is used. Drain pancakes on paper towel.

3 To make Cilantro Mayonnaise: Combine mayonnaise, lime juice, cilantro and scallions in bowl. Mix well. Add pepper to taste. Serve pancakes hot or cool with a dollop of Cilantro Mayonnaise.

COOK'S FILE

Storage time: Cilantro Mayonnaise can be made up to one day in advance. Store, covered, in refrigerator. Corn pancakes can be made several hours in advance. Reheat gently just before serving.
Variation: Frozen corn kernels can be used in place of canned corn.

SWEET POTATO MUFFINS

Preparation time: 15 minutes
Total cooking time: 25 minutes +
   10 minutes cooling
Makes 12

6 oz sweet potato
2 cups all-purpose flour
1¹/2 teaspoons baking powder
¹/2 teaspoon baking soda
¹/4 teaspoon salt
1 cup finely grated cheddar cheese
¹/3 cup butter, melted and cooled
1 egg, lightly beaten
³/4 cup buttermilk
salt and freshly ground black
   pepper to taste

➤ PREHEAT OVEN to moderate 350°F. Brush melted butter or oil into 12 deep muffin tins.

1 Finely grate potato. Sift flour, baking powder, baking soda and salt into bowl. Add potato and cheese, stir to combine. Make a well in the center.

2 Add butter, egg and buttermilk all at once to well. Stir until just combined.

3 Spoon mixture into prepared muffin tins. Bake for 25 minutes, until puffed and lightly golden. Turn onto a wire rack to cool for 10 minutes before serving. Serve warm with butter.

COOK'S FILE

Storage time: Muffins are best eaten on the day they are made.

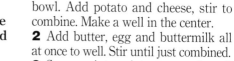

SAVORY TARTS

Preparation time: 40 minutes
Total cooking time: 15–20 minutes
Makes 20

¹/4 cup butter, melted
1 clove garlic, crushed
20 slices white bread

Filling
1 large carrot
1 large zucchini
1 tablespoon oil
1 teaspoon grated ginger
2 scallions, finely sliced
³/4 cup cauliflower, cut in small
   florets
1 tablespoon wholegrain
   mustard
¹/2 teaspoon dried basil
2 tablespoons chopped fresh
   chives
salt and freshly ground black
   pepper to taste

➤ PREHEAT OVEN to moderate 350°F. Brush two 12-cup shallow muffin tins with melted butter or oil.

1 Cut carrot and zucchini into short thin strips.

2 Combine butter and garlic in small bowl. Remove crusts from bread with a sharp knife. Using a rolling pin, flatten each slice of bread. Cut bread slices into rounds, using a 2 inch plain or fluted cutter. Brush bread with butter mixture. Place bread rounds into the prepared tins, press firmly. Bake for 10 minutes or until golden and crisp. Transfer to wire rack to cool.

3 To make Filling: Heat oil in medium heavy-based frying pan. Add ginger and scallions, cook over medium heat 1 minute. Add carrot, zucchini and cauliflower. Cook a further 5 minutes or until vegetables are tender. Add mustard, basil and chives, season to taste and stir until combined. Remove from heat. Spoon one tablespoon of the vegetable filling into each tart case. Sprinkle with extra chopped chives. Serve warm or cold.

COOK'S FILE

Storage time: Tart cases can be prepared and cooked one day in advance. Store in an airtight container. Prepare the filling and fill cases just before serving.

Variation: Use wholewheat or wholegrain bread in place of white.

*Sweet Potato Muffins (top)
and Savory Tarts.*

1

2

3

4

VEGETABLE WONTONS WITH CHILI SAUCE

Preparation time: 40 minutes + 30 minutes soaking
Total cooking time: 20 minutes
Makes 25

8 dried Chinese mushrooms
1 tablespoon peanut oil
1 teaspoon sesame oil
1 teaspoon grated ginger
2 scallions, finely chopped
1 medium carrot, finely chopped
1 medium parsnip, finely chopped
3 oz broccoli, cut into small florets
2 tablespoons bread crumbs
1 tablespoon soy sauce
2 tablespoons water
25 wonton wrappers
oil for deep frying

Chili Sauce
1 tablespoon peanut oil
1 clove garlic, crushed
1/4 cup sweet chili sauce
2 tablespoons soy sauce
2 tablespoons sherry
1 tablespoon lemon juice

➤ SOAK MUSHROOMS in hot water to cover for 30 minutes.

1 Drain mushrooms, squeeze to remove excess liquid. Remove stems, discard. Shred mushroom caps finely.

2 Heat oils in wok or heavy-based frying pan. Add ginger and scallions. Cook 1 minute over medium heat. Add mushrooms, carrot, parsnip and broccoli and stir-fry for 3 minutes or until vegetables are just softened. Add bread crumbs, soy sauce and water, stirring to combine. Remove from heat; cool.

3 Work with one wonton wrapper at a time, keeping the remainder covered with a damp dish towel to prevent them drying out. Place a heaped teaspoonful of vegetable mixture in the center of each round. Moisten the edges of pastry with water, and pinch edges together to seal. Repeat procedure with remaining wrappers and filling. Heat the oil in a wok or deep-fryer. Cook wontons in batches (no more than four at a time), for 2 minutes or until golden and crisp. Remove with tongs or a slotted spoon. Drain on paper towels. Serve immediately with Chili Sauce.

4 To make Chili Sauce: Heat oil in a small pan, add garlic. Cook until just golden. Add chili and soy sauces, sherry and juice, stir until smooth and heated through.

COOK'S FILE

Storage time: Vegetable mixture for wontons can be prepared up to Step 3, one day in advance. Store, covered, in refrigerator. Assemble and cook just before serving.

Hint: Wonton wrappers are available at Chinese food stores and the produce section of some supermarkets.

VEGETABLE FRITTERS WITH TOMATO SAUCE

Preparation time: 30 minutes
Total cooking time: 36 minutes
Makes 12

2 medium potatoes, peeled
1 medium carrot, peeled
2 medium zucchini
4 oz sweet potato, peeled
1 small leek
2 tablespoons all-purpose flour
3 eggs, lightly beaten
oil for frying

Fresh Tomato Sauce
1 tablespoon oil

1 small onion, finely chopped
1 clove garlic, crushed
1/2 teaspoon ground paprika
3 ripe medium tomatoes, finely chopped
1/4 cup finely shredded fresh basil

➤ FINELY GRATE potatoes, carrot, zucchini and sweet potato. Finely slice leek (white part only).

1 Cup small handfuls of grated vegetables in both hands and squeeze out as much excess moisture as possible. Place into a large mixing bowl with leek, and combine well.

2 Sprinkle flour over vegetables, and combine. Add eggs and mix well. Heat about 1/4 inch of oil in a frying pan,

and drop in 1/4 cup of mixture in a neat pile. Use a fork to gently form mixture into a 4 inch round. Fry two to three at a time for 3 minutes each side over medium heat until golden and crispy. Drain on paper towel; keep warm. Repeat with remaining mixture.

3 To make Tomato Sauce: Heat oil in a small pan. Add onion, garlic and paprika; cook over medium heat 3 minutes or until soft. Add tomatoes, reduce heat to low, and cook 10 minutes, stirring occasionally. Stir in basil. Serve warm.

COOK'S FILE

Storage time: Make fritters just before serving. Tomato Sauce can be made up to eight hours in advance.

ZUCCHINI FINGERS

Preparation time: 40 minutes
Total cooking time: 25 minutes
Makes 18 fingers

1 package frozen puff pastry
    sheets, thawed
1 egg, lightly beaten
8 oz cream cheese, softened
1 tablespoon mayonnaise
2 oz sundried tomatoes in oil,
    well drained and chopped
1 clove garlic, crushed
1 teaspoon dried basil leaves
6 medium zucchini
1/4 cup olive oil
1 tablespoon lemon juice
2 tablespoons black olive paste

➤ PREHEAT OVEN to moderately hot 375°F. Brush two baking pans with melted butter or oil.

1 Cut three puff pastry sheets into 3 x 9½ inch strips. Cut remaining pastry into ½ x 9½ inch strips. Brush pastry strips with egg. Place one thin strip of pastry down each side of the larger strip to form an edge. Prick pastry well with a fork. Place on prepared pans. Bake 15 minutes or until crisp and golden. Cool on wire rack. Using electric beaters, beat cream cheese until light and creamy. Add mayonnaise, tomatoes, garlic and basil; beat until well combined. Set aside.

2 Cut ends from zucchini. Cut zucchini in thin slices lengthwise. Place on cold broiler rack. Brush with olive oil.

Broil 5 inches from heat 10 minutes or until golden brown. Drain on paper towel. Drizzle with lemon juice.

3 Spread pastry shells with olive paste. Top with cheese mixture, smooth surface. Arrange overlapping slices of zucchini over cheese. Cut each into six fingers to serve.

COOK'S FILE

Storage time: Cream cheese filling can be prepared one day in advance. Store, covered, in refrigerator. Fingers can be cooked and assembled up to two hours before serving.

Hint: Olive paste is available from specialty food stores and supermarkets. If unavailable, make your own using pitted black olives and a small amount of olive oil. Process until smooth.

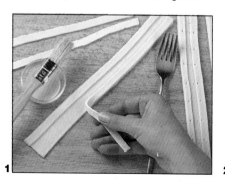

1

2

3

CRISP POTATO SKINS WITH CHILI CHEESE DIP

Preparation time: 30 minutes
Total cooking time: 1 hour 15 minutes
Serves 4–6

6 medium potatoes
oil for shallow frying

Chili Cheese Dip
1 tablespoon oil
1 small onion, finely chopped
1 clove garlic, crushed
1 teaspoon mild chili
    powder
3/4 cup sour cream
2 cups grated cheddar cheese

➤ PREHEAT OVEN to moderately hot 375°F.

1 Scrub potatoes and dry thoroughly; do not peel. Prick each potato twice with a fork. Bake for 1 hour, until skins are crisp and flesh is soft when pierced with a knife. Turn once during cooking. Remove from oven and cool.

2 Cut potatoes in half and scoop out flesh, leaving about 1/4 inch of potato in the shell. Set aside flesh for another use. Cut each half into three wedges.

3 Heat oil in a medium heavy-based pan. Gently place batches of potato skins into moderately hot oil. Cook for 1–2 minutes or until golden and crispy. Drain on paper towels. Serve immediately with Chili Cheese Dip.

4 To make Chili Cheese Dip: Heat oil in a small pan. Add onion and cook over a medium heat 2 minutes or until soft. Add garlic and chili powder, cook 1 minute, stirring. Add sour cream and stir until it is warm and thinned down slightly; add cheese and stir until melted and mixture is almost smooth. Serve hot.

COOK'S FILE

Storage time: Potatoes may be baked and prepared for frying up to eight hours in advance. Fry just before serving. Prepare Chili Cheese Dip just before serving.

Variation: Cut the whole baked potatoes into wedges, fry and serve as described above.

Purchased chili potato chips could be served with this dip.

SPINACH AND OLIVE BITES

Preparation time: 1 hour + 1 hour
    refrigeration
Total cooking time: 15 minutes
Makes 30

2 cups all-purpose flour
1/4 teaspoon salt
3/4 cup butter, cut into 1/4 inch
    cubes
3/4 cup water

Filling
2 oz spinach leaves
4 oz feta cheese
2 tablespoons chopped pitted
    black olives
2 teaspoons chopped fresh
    rosemary
1 clove garlic, crushed
2 tablespoons pistachio nuts
1 egg, lightly beaten

➤ SIFT FLOUR and salt into a large mixing bowl; stir in cubed butter until just combined.

1 Make a well in the center of the flour, add almost all the water. Mix to a slightly sticky dough with a knife, adding more water if necessary. Gather dough into a ball.

2 Turn onto a well-floured surface, and lightly press together until almost smooth. Do not overwork dough. Roll out to a neat 8 x 16 inch rectangle, trying to keep the corners fairly square. Fold the top third of the pastry down and fold the bottom third of the pastry up over it. Make a quarter turn to the right so that the edge of the top fold is on the right. Re-roll pastry to a 8 x 16 inch rectangle, and repeat folding step. Wrap pastry in plastic wrap and refrigerate for 30 minutes.

3 Repeat previous step, giving a roll,

fold and turn twice more. Refrigerate for another 30 minutes. The folding and rolling give the pastry its flaky characteristics. Roll out pastry on a well-floured surface to a 1/8 inch thickness, and cut out thirty 3 inch rounds.

4 Preheat oven to moderate 350°F. Brush a large baking sheet with melted butter or oil. Wash and dry spinach leaves thoroughly. Shred spinach finely, place in medium mixing bowl. Crumble feta over spinach, add olives, rosemary and garlic.

5 Spread pistachios on a baking sheet and toast under a broiler 5–6 inches from heat for 1–2 minutes. Cool and chop finely. Add to spinach mixture with egg, stir until well combined.

6 Place two teaspoonfuls of mixture in the center of each round, fold in half and pinch edges to seal. Place on prepared baking sheet, brush lightly with beaten egg and bake for 15 minutes, until golden and crisp. Serve hot.

COOK'S FILE

Storage time: Flaky pastry can be made up to one day in advance. Store in refrigerator. Assemble bites and cook just before serving.

Hints: Homemade flaky pastry is delicious and well worth the effort if time permits. When making flaky pastry, have ingredients, equipment and room temperature as cool as possible. If too warm, butter in pastry will melt and it will be difficult to work with.

Variation: Frozen puff pastry may be substituted in this recipe. Use ready-rolled sheets of frozen, thawed puff pastry for best results.

Note: Feta cheese is available from delicatessens and supermarkets. It is a dry white cheese, cured in brine. The Bulgarian and Greek varieties are strongest in flavor. Originally made from goats' or ewes' milk, nowadays it is often made from cows' milk.

1

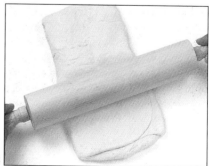

3

VEGETABLE SAMOSAS

Preparation time: 20 minutes
Total cooking time: 30 minutes
Makes 32

1 tablespoon ghee or oil
1 small onion, finely chopped
1 clove garlic, crushed
2 teaspoons grated fresh ginger
1 teaspoon mustard seeds
1 teaspoon ground cumin
1/2 teaspoon ground turmeric
1/4 teaspoon chili powder
10 oz potatoes, peeled
3/4 cup water
1/2 cup frozen peas
2 tablespoons chopped fresh
    cilantro
salt to taste
4 sheets refrigerated unbaked
    piecrusts (2 packages)
oil for deep frying

Yogurt Dip
1/2 small cucumber
1 cup plain yogurt
2 tablespoons finely chopped
    fresh mint

➤ HEAT GHEE or oil in medium pan, add onion, garlic and ginger. Cook over low heat 5 minutes, until onion is soft. Add spices, cook 1 minute.

1 Cut potatoes into 1/4 inch cubes. Add to pan, stir to combine. Add water, cover and cook 5–10 minutes until potatoes are just tender, stirring occasionally. Drain.

2 Remove pan from heat and stir in peas, cilantro and salt; cool.

3 Cut 61/2 x 41/2 inch pastry circles; cut each in half. Fold each semicircle in half; pinch straight sides together to form cones. Spoon 2 teaspoons of filling into each cone. Pinch edge to seal. Heat oil in a medium pan. Cook samosas in batches in moderately hot oil 2–3 minutes until crisp and golden. Drain on paper towels. Serve warm with Yogurt Dip.

4 To make Yogurt Dip: Peel cucumber, remove seeds and finely chop flesh. Combine with yogurt and mint in a small bowl.

COOK'S FILE

Storage time: Filling can be made one day in advance. Assemble and cook just before serving.

1

2

3

4

AVOCADO SALSA

Preparation time: 15 minutes
Total cooking time: 1 minute
Serves 6

1 medium red onion
2 large avocados
1/4 teaspoon lime juice
1 medium tomato
1 small red pepper
1 teaspoon ground coriander
1 teaspoon ground cumin
1/4 cup chopped fresh cilantro
    leaves
2 tablespoons olive oil
4–5 drops Tabasco

➤ FINELY CHOP the red onion.
1 Cut avocados in half, remove pit and carefully peel. Finely chop flesh, place in a medium mixing bowl and toss lightly with lime juice.
2 Cut tomato in half horizontally and squeeze gently to remove seeds; chop finely. Remove seeds and membrane from pepper, chop finely.
3 Place the ground coriander and cumin in a small pan, stir over medium heat 1 minute to enhance fragrance and flavor; cool. Add all ingredients to avocado in bowl and gently combine, so that the avocado retains its shape and is not mashed. Refrigerate until required, serve at room temperature with corn chips.

C O O K ' S   F I L E

Storage time: This dish can be made up to four hours in advance.
Hint: For immediate use, choose an avocado that will just give to a gentle squeeze. Avocados should have skin without blemishes or brown patches. Green-skinned varieties should have shiny skins. Over-ripe avocados are sometimes offered at a low price, but on opening can be rancid and brown. Better still, buy avocados that are just underripe, and check them daily to use at their peak. Storing avocados with bananas will hasten the ripening process. Place avocados in a brown paper bag on top of the refrigerator to ripen them overnight.

QUICK ONE-STEP RECIPES

Simple, time-saving methods that bring out the best in vegetables. These recipes make both hot and cold dishes with the minimum of fuss and bother – just what the modern cook ordered. All recipes make four servings.

Carrots

HONEY-GLAZED CARROTS

Peel and cut 2 medium carrots into thin diagonal slices. Steam or microwave until just tender. Do not overcook. Drain excess liquid from pan. Add 1 tablespoon butter and 1–2 teaspoons honey. Toss until well combined and the butter has melted. Sprinkle with chopped fresh chives or chopped fresh parsley. Serve hot.

CARROT RIBBONS

Trim the ends from 3 medium carrots. Peel carrots lengthwise into strips using a sharp vegetable peeler. Heat 2 tablespoons butter in medium heavy-based frying pan. Add 1 teaspoon brown sugar and the carrot ribbons. Toss until well coated with butter, and carrots are tender but still crisp. Do not overcook. Add 1 tablespoon freshly chopped cilantro leaves. Drizzle sparingly with balsamic vinegar if desired. Serve hot.

HERBED CARROT STICKS

Peel and cut 3 medium carrots into thin matchstick lengths. Steam or microwave until just tender. Do not overcook. Add 2 tablespoons butter and 1 tablespoon finely chopped fresh herbs or 2 teaspoons dried mixed herbs. Toss until well coated and butter has melted. Season to taste with salt and freshly ground black pepper. Serve hot.

GARLIC BUTTERED BABY CARROTS

Trim 12 baby (Dutch) carrots. Steam or microwave until just tender. Do not overcook. Heat 2 tablespoons butter in a medium pan. Add 2 cloves crushed garlic, 1/2 teaspoon sugar and 1 teaspoon finely grated lemon rind. Cook for 1 minute. Add carrots, stir until well coated and heated through. Sprinkle with finely chopped fresh herbs to taste. Serve hot.

Clockwise from top: Garlic Buttered Baby Carrots, Herbed Carrot Sticks, Carrot Ribbons, Honey-glazed Carrots.

**FRENCH FRIES
OR CURLS**

GOLDEN ROASTED POTATOES

Potatoes

CREAMY POTATO

FRENCH FRIES OR CURLS

Peel 4 medium potatoes. Cut lengthwise into 1/2 inch thick slices, then into 1/2 inch wide sticks or peel long potato strips with a vegetable peeler. Cook in a deep pan of moderately hot oil for 4–5 minutes for fries, 2–3 minutes for curls, or until golden and crisp. Drain on paper towels. Serve hot.

GOLDEN ROASTED POTATOES

Peel 4 medium potatoes. Place in baking dish, brush liberally with combined 1 tablespoon olive oil and 2 tablespoons melted butter. Bake at moderately hot 375°F for 20 minutes, brush with oil mixture. Bake further 30 minutes or until crisp and golden. Serve hot.

CREAMY POTATO

Peel and chop 4 medium potatoes. Cook in a large pan of boiling water until just tender; drain and mash. Add 2 tablespoons butter and 2–3 tablespoons cream. Season to taste with salt and pepper. Stir until smooth and creamy. Sprinkle with chopped fresh herbs. Serve hot.

DUCHESS POTATOES

Peel and chop 4 medium potatoes. Cook in a large pan of boiling water until just tender; drain and mash. Add 3 egg yolks, 2 tablespoons cream and 2 tablespoons grated Parmesan cheese. Mix thoroughly. Pipe mixture into swirls onto greased baking pans. Bake in moderately hot oven 375°F for 20 minutes or until golden brown. Sprinkle with paprika. Serve hot.

DUCHESS POTATOES

**QUICK CHEESY
POTATO BAKE**

QUICK CHEESY POTATO BAKE

Peel and thinly slice 4 medium potatoes. Thinly slice 1 onion. Layer potato and onion slices in an ovenproof baking dish. Sprinkle grated cheddar cheese between each layer. Pour over combined 1/2 cup cream, 3/4 cup milk and 1 teaspoon mustard powder. Sprinkle top with extra grated cheese and chopped chives. Bake in moderate oven 375°F for 40 minutes or until cooked. Serve hot.

HERBED NEW POTATOES

Wash 12 small new potatoes. Cook in a large pan of boiling water until tender; tip into a colander to drain. Toss with 1/4 cup melted butter and 2 teaspoons each of freshly chopped basil and chives or parsley. Serve hot.

HERBED NEW POTATOES

POTATO SALAD

Peel and chop 4 medium potatoes into 1/2 inch cubes. Cook in a medium pan of boiling water until just tender; drain. Rinse and drain again; leave to cool. Combine 3/4 cup whole egg mayonnaise, 2 chopped scallions, 1 chopped stalk celery, 2 teaspoons lemon juice and 1 slice bacon, cooked and finely chopped. Mix well. Add potatoes. Toss through, serve. Add extra chopped herbs if desired. Cover and refrigerate. Serve cold.

HASSELBACK POTATOES

Peel and halve 4 medium potatoes. Place potatoes cut-side down. Use a sharp knife to make thin slices in potatoes, taking care not to cut right through. Place potatoes cut-side-up in baking dish. Brush with 1 tablespoon olive oil combined with 20 g melted butter. Sprinkle with lemon pepper. Bake in moderately hot 210°C/190°C gas oven for 45 minutes or until golden and slightly crisp. Serve immediately.

HASSELBACK POTATOES

POTATO SALAD

Broccoli

BROCCOLI WITH CHEESE SAUCE

Cut 8 oz broccoli into small florets. Steam until just tender. Heat 3 tablespoons butter in medium pan; add 2 tablespoons all-purpose flour. Stir over low heat 2 minutes or until lightly golden and bubbling. Gradually add 1 cup milk, stirring until smooth. Stir constantly over medium heat until mixture boils and thickens. Take off heat; stir through 1/3 cup grated cheddar cheese until melted. Pour over hot broccoli to serve.

BROCCOLI WITH CASHEWS

Cut 8 oz broccoli into small florets. Heat 1 tablespoon olive oil in heavy-based frying pan. Add 1 clove crushed garlic and 1/2 cup cashew nuts (unsalted). Stir over medium heat 2 minutes or until lightly golden. Add broccoli, stir-fry for 3–4 minutes or until just tender. Serve hot.

BROCCOLI WITH BACON AND PINE NUTS

Cut 8 oz broccoli into small florets. Heat 2 teaspoons oil in wok or heavy-based frying pan. Add 2 pieces of Canadian bacon, sliced into strips. Cook over medium heat 2 minutes. Add broccoli, stir-fry 3–4 minutes until just tender. Stir in 2 tablespoons toasted pine nuts and 1 tablespoon chopped fresh chives. Serve hot.

BROCCOLI WITH CHEESE SAUCE

BROCCOLI WITH CASHEWS

BROCCOLI WITH BACON AND PINE NUTS

BROCCOLI AND ONION STIR-FRY

BROCCOLI AND ONION STIR-FRY

Cut 8 oz broccoli into small florets. Slice a medium onion into 8 wedges. Heat 2 teaspoons sesame oil and 2 teaspoons vegetable oil in wok or frying pan. Add broccoli and onions, cook until just tender. Stir in 2 teaspoons soy sauce and 1 tablespoon sweet chili sauce. Sprinkle with herbs. Serve.

BUTTERED BROCCOLI AND HERBS

Cut 8 oz broccoli into small florets. Heat 3 tablespoons butter in wok or heavy-based frying pan. Add broccoli. Cover and cook over medium heat until just tender. Stir through 1/4 cup mixed chopped fresh herbs. (Use any combination: basil, mint, chives, parsley, oregano, marjoram, thyme, cilantro or dill). Serve hot.

LEMON BROCCOLI

Cut 8 oz broccoli into small florets. Steam broccoli until just tender. Toss broccoli in 2 teaspoons olive oil combined with 1 tablespoon lemon juice. Serve hot.

BROCCOLI AND MUSHROOMS

Cut 8 oz broccoli into small florets. Heat 2 tablespoons butter and 1 clove crushed garlic in heavy-based frying pan. Add 4 sliced button mushrooms. Cook over medium heat 2 minutes or until tender. Remove from pan, set aside. Add broccoli, stir-fry 3–4 minutes until tender. Return mushrooms to pan, stir until heated through. Serve hot.

BROCCOLI WITH MUSTARD BUTTER

Cut 8 oz broccoli into medium florets. Steam broccoli until just tender. Combine 1/4 cup softened butter, 2 teaspoons Dijon mustard and freshly ground black pepper to taste. Mix well. Serve over hot broccoli.

BUTTERED BROCCOLI AND HERBS

LEMON BROCCOLI

BROCCOLI AND MUSHROOMS

BROCCOLI WITH MUSTARD BUTTER

CABBAGE AND SCALLION STIR-FRY

SWEET RED CABBAGE WITH CARAWAY SEEDS

SAUTEED CABBAGE

QUICK COLESLAW

Cabbage

SWEET RED CABBAGE WITH CARAWAY SEEDS

Finely shred 1/2 small red cabbage. Heat 2 tablespoons butter, 1 teaspoon caraway seeds, 1 teaspoon balsamic vinegar and 1 teaspoon brown sugar in a large frying pan. Add cabbage, cook, stirring, 2–3 minutes or until just tender. Serve hot.

SAUTEED CABBAGE

Finely shred 1/2 small green cabbage. Heat 2 tablespoons butter, 1 clove crushed garlic and 2 slices finely shredded ham or bacon in large pan. Cook 1 minute, add cabbage. Cook, stirring, 2–3 minutes or until cabbage is just tender. Serve hot.

CABBAGE AND SCALLION STIR-FRY

Finely shred 1/2 small green cabbage. Heat 2 teaspoons olive oil and 2 tablespoons butter in heavy-based frying pan or wok. Add cabbage and 2 finely sliced scallions. Stir-fry 2–3 minutes or until just tender. Serve hot.

QUICK COLESLAW

Finely shred 1/2 small green cabbage. Combine with 2 grated carrots, 1 stalk finely chopped celery stalk, 1 finely chopped onion, 1 finely chopped small green or red pepper and 1/2 cup prepared coleslaw dressing in a large bowl. Toss well to combine. Add 1/4 cup mixed freshly chopped herbs if desired. Chill before serving.

CABBAGE AND BEANS

GARLIC PEPPER CABBAGE

SWEET CHILI CABBAGE

CABBAGE AND POTATO CAKES

SWEET CHILLI CABBAGE

Finely shred 1/2 small Chinese or green cabbage. Heat 2 teaspoons sesame oil in frying pan or wok. Add 2–3 teaspoons sweet chili sauce, 1 teaspoon soy sauce and cabbage. Stir-fry 2–3 minutes or until just tender. Serve hot.

CABBAGE AND POTATO CAKES

Combine 1 cup cooked cabbage, 1/2 cup roughly mashed potato, 1 finely chopped scallion, 2 lightly beaten eggs and salt and freshly ground pepper to taste and mix well. Heat oil or butter in frying pan. Cook spoonfuls of mixture in batches 2 minutes each side or until golden. Drain on paper towels. Serve hot.

GARLIC PEPPER CABBAGE

Finely shred 1/2 small green cabbage. Heat 2 tablespoons butter and 1 teaspoon oil in heavy-based frying pan or wok. Add 1–2 teaspoons garlic pepper seasoning and cabbage. Stir-fry 2–3 minutes or until just tender. Serve hot.

CABBAGE AND BEANS

Finely shred 1/2 small green or red cabbage. Heat 1 tablespoon olive oil in frying pan or wok. Add 1 clove crushed garlic, 1/4 teaspoon sugar, 12 finely shredded green beans and cabbage. Stir-fry 3–4 minutes or until vegetables are just tender. Serve hot, sprinkled with cracked or freshly ground black pepper to taste.

Squash

CANDIED SQUASH

Peel and cut 1 lb winter squash in thin slices. Lay slices overlapping in ovenproof dish. Heat 3 tablespoons butter, 2 tablespoons cream and 1 tablespoon brown sugar in a small pan on low heat. Stir until smooth. Pour over squash. Bake in moderate 350°F oven for 35 minutes or until squash is tender. Serve sprinkled with chopped chives.

BAKED SQUASH

Peel 1 lb winter squash. Cut into large pieces. Place in baking dish. Brush liberally with combined 2 tablespoons melted butter and 2 teaspoons olive oil. Bake in moderate 350°F oven 40 minutes or until dark golden and cooked through.

SQUASH AND NUTMEG PUREE

Peel 1 lb winter squash. Cut into pieces. Steam or microwave until soft. Mash with a fork or potato masher. Add ¼ teaspoon ground nutmeg, 2 tablespoons butter and salt and pepper. Stir until smooth. Spoon or pipe onto plate.

SQUASH WITH CHIVE BUTTER

Peel 1 lb winter squash. Cut into ⅔ inch cubes. Steam or microwave until just tender. Combine 3 tablespoons softened butter, 1 tablespoon chopped chives and freshly ground black pepper to taste. Serve on hot squash.

CANDIED SQUASH

BAKED SQUASH

SQUASH AND NUTMEG PUREE

PUMPKIN WITH CHIVE BUTTER

SQUASH WITH GARLIC AND HERB BUTTER

SWEET SPICED SQUASH

FRIED SQUASH RIBBONS

PUMPKIN SOUP

SQUASH WITH GARLIC AND HERB BUTTER

Peel 1 lb winter squash. Cut into thin slices. Steam or microwave until tender. Combine 3 tablespoons softened butter, 1 clove crushed garlic, 2 teaspoons chopped fresh cilantro leaves, 2 teaspoons chopped fresh mint. Mix well. Pipe rosettes onto paper-lined tray. Refrigerate until firm. Serve on hot squash.

SWEET SPICED SQUASH

Peel 1 lb winter squash. Cut into thin slices. Place on a greased foil-lined baking pan. Melt 3 tablespoons butter. Brush over squash. Combine 1/2 teaspoon each ground cumin, ground coriander, ground ginger and 1 teaspoon brown sugar. Mix well and sprinkle over squash. Bake in moderate 350°F oven 35 minutes or until cooked through. Serve hot.

SQUASH SOUP

Place 2 cups of cooked, mashed winter squash, 2 tablespoons butter, 1/2 cup chicken stock, 2 roughly chopped scallions and 1/2 cup milk in food processor bowl. Using the pulse action, process until smooth. Transfer mixture to large pan, stir in 1/2 cup cream. Season with salt and pepper. Heat through. Serve hot with sour cream and a sprinkle of ground nutmeg.

FRIED SQUASH RIBBONS

Peel 1 lb winter squash. Peel squash into ribbons using a vegetable peeler. Heat a medium pan half filled with oil. Deep-fry squash ribbons in batches until crisp and golden. Drain on paper towels. Sprinkle with salt and pepper to taste. Serve hot.

Spinach

SHREDDED SPINACH AND BACON

Finely shred 1 bunch spinach. Cut 2 bacon slices in thin strips. Heat 2 teaspoons olive oil in frying pan. Add bacon, fry on medium-high heat until almost crisp. Add spinach, toss through until just wilted. Serve hot.

SPINACH WITH VINAIGRETTE

Finely shred 1 bunch spinach. Combine 2 tablespoons olive oil, 2 teaspoons seeded mustard, 1 tablespoon balsamic vinegar, 1 clove crushed garlic, 1/2 teaspoon brown sugar and freshly ground black pepper to taste. Mix well, pour dressing over spinach, toss lightly. Serve cool.

SPINACH AND BUTTERED CHIVES

Finely shred 1 bunch spinach. Place in a mixing bowl. Heat 2 tablespoons butter and 1 tablespoon oil in a small pan. Add 1/4 cup finely chopped chives and 1 teaspoon cracked black pepper. Cook 1 minute. Add to spinach in bowl, mix well. Serve immediately.

CREAMED SPINACH

Tear 1 bunch spinach into pieces. Heat 2 tablespoons butter in heavy-based frying pan. Add 1 finely sliced small onion. Cook 2–3 minutes or until onion is soft. Add spinach, cook 1 minute. Stir in 1/4 cup cream, heat through. Sprinkle with nutmeg and grated cheddar cheese. Serve hot.

SPINACH AND BUTTERED CHIVES

SHREDDED SPINACH AND BACON

SPINACH WITH VINAIGRETTE

CREAMED SPINACH

SWEET CHILI SPINACH SALAD

Finely shred 1 bunch spinach. Heat 1 tablespoon sesame oil, 2 teaspoons soy sauce, 1 tablespoon chili sauce and 1 teaspoon fish sauce in a small pan. Cook 1 minute. Add 2 tablespoons freshly chopped cilantro leaves. Toss through spinach to combine. Serve cool.

**SWEET CHILI
SPINACH SALAD**

SPINACH AND SCALLION SALAD

Tear 1 bunch spinach leaves into pieces. Combine in bowl with 2–3 finely shredded scallions. Season with salt and freshly ground black pepper to taste. Drizzle with 1 tablespoon olive oil combined with 1–2 tablespoons red wine or balsamic vinegar. Serve cool.

BASIL SPINACH SALAD

Tear 1 bunch spinach into pieces. Combine in bowl with 1/4 cup shredded basil leaves and 2 tablespoons toasted pine nuts. Finely slice 1 bacon slice. Cook in small pan until crisp. Combine 2 tablespoons oil, 1 tablespoon white wine vinegar, 1 tablespoon sour cream, 1/2 teaspoon sugar and 1 clove crushed garlic. Mix well and drizzle over salad. Top with bacon and Parmesan cheese shavings. Serve cool.

EGGS FLORENTINE

Tear 2 bunches spinach into pieces. Steam or microwave until tender. Combine spinach with 2 tablespoons butter, a pinch of nutmeg and salt to taste. Divide mixture into 2 ramekin dishes. Top each with a poached egg. Sprinkle with grated cheddar cheese. Bake in moderate 350°F oven for 5–10 minutes until cheese melts and browns. Serve hot.

BASIL SPINACH SALAD

**SPINACH AND SPRING
ONION SALAD**

EGGS FLORENTINE

39

Beans

GARLIC AND BASIL BEANS

Top and tail 20 green beans. Heat 1 tablespoon olive oil in frying pan or wok. Add 1 clove crushed garlic and beans. Cook, stirring, 2–3 minutes or until beans are just tender. Stir in 1 tablespoon shredded basil leaves. Serve hot.

PEPPER BEANS AND HAM

Top and tail 20 green beans. Heat 1 tablespoon olive oil in frying pan or wok. Add 2 slices finely sliced ham and 1 teaspoon cracked black pepper. Cook 1 minute. Add beans, stir-fry 2–3 minutes or until beans are just tender. Serve hot.

BEANS HOLLANDAISE

Top and tail 20 green beans. Steam until just tender. Place 2 egg yolks in food processor bowl. Process 10 seconds or until yolk is blended. With motor constantly running, add 1/2 cup melted butter in a thin stream until mixture is thick and creamy, then add 1 tablespoon lemon juice. Season with salt and freshly ground black pepper to taste. Spoon over warm beans. Serve immediately.

BEANS AND CASHEWS

Top and tail 20 green beans. Cut into 1½ inch diagonal lengths. Heat 2 teaspoons sesame oil in frying pan or wok. Add 1 clove crushed garlic and 1/3 cup cashew nuts. Cook 2 minutes. Add beans, stir-fry 2–3 minutes or until nuts are golden and beans just tender. Serve hot.

BEANS HOLLANDAISE

GARLIC AND BASIL BEANS

BEANS AND CASHEWS

PEPPER BEANS AND HAM

BEAN BUNDLES

BEAN BUNDLES

Top and tail 20 green beans. Divide beans into bundles of five. Tie together with a scallion green or chives. Steam or microwave until just tender. Sprinkle with lemon pepper. Serve hot.

BEAN AND WALNUT SALAD

Finely shred 20 green beans. Combine in a bowl with 1/4 cup cilantro leaves, 4 large red leaf lettuce leaves torn in pieces, 1/4 finely shredded red pepper, 1/3 cup walnut halves, 2 tablespoons tarragon vinegar, 1–2 tablespoons peanut oil and 2 tablespoons chopped fresh mint. Mix well. Serve immediately.

BEANS IN HERB CREAM SAUCE

Top and tail 20 green beans. Heat 2 tablespoons butter in frying pan or wok. Add 1 clove crushed garlic and beans. Cook 2–3 minutes or until just tender. Stir in 1/4 cup cream, 2 teaspoons chopped fresh rosemary, 1 tablespoon chopped fresh chives and 1 teaspoon chopped fresh thyme. Cook 1 minute more. Serve hot.

MINTED TOMATO AND BEANS

Cut 20 green beans in half diagonally. Heat 1 teaspoon oil in frying pan. Add 1 clove crushed garlic, 1 teaspoon grated ginger, 1/2 teaspoon each of ground coriander, cumin and garam masala, 2 chopped ripe tomatoes. Cook, stirring, for 1 minute. Add beans, cook 2–3 minutes or until just tender. Stir in 1 tablespoon chopped fresh mint. Serve hot.

BEAN AND WALNUT SALAD

BEANS IN HERB CREAM SAUCE

MINTED TOMATO AND BEANS

CURRIED ONION RINGS

SPICY ONIONS AND TOMATOES

GOLDEN BABY ONIONS

GARLIC ONIONS

Onions

SPICY ONIONS AND TOMATOES

Peel and thinly slice 2 medium red onions. Heat 2 table-spoons butter, 1 tablespoon oil, $1/2$ teaspoon each ground cumin, coriander, turmeric and garam masala. Add onions, cook 2–3 minutes. Stir in 2 chopped medium ripe tomatoes. Cook 3 minutes more or until onions are soft. Serve hot, sprinkled with chopped cilantro.

GOLDEN BABY ONIONS

Peel 12 small onions, leaving base intact. Heat 2 table-spoons butter, 1 tablespoon oil and $1/4$ teaspoon ground sweet paprika in frying pan or wok. Add onions. Cook over medium heat 5 minutes or until onions are golden brown and tender, stir in $1/2$ teaspoon brown sugar. Serve hot.

CURRIED ONION RINGS

Peel and cut 2 medium onions into thin rings. Heat 2 tablespoons olive oil in frying pan. Add 2 teaspoons curry powder and onions. Cook 5 minutes or until onions are tender. Stir in $1/2$ teaspoon brown sugar. Serve hot.

GARLIC ONIONS

Peel and cut 2 medium onions into eight wedges. Heat 1 tablespoon butter and 2 tablespoons oil in frying pan. Add 1–2 cloves crushed garlic and onions. Cook over medium heat 5–6 minutes or until tender. Sprinkle with chopped chives.

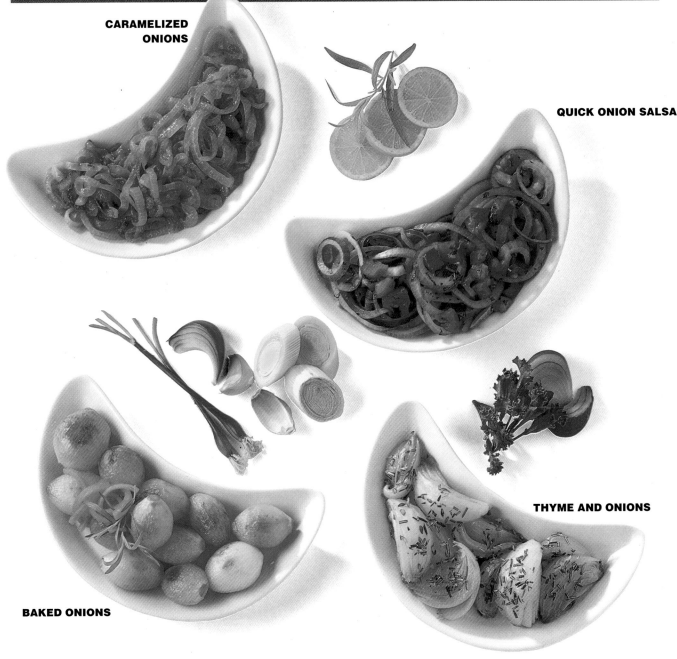

CARAMELIZED ONIONS

QUICK ONION SALSA

BAKED ONIONS

THYME AND ONIONS

CARAMELIZED ONIONS

Peel and cut 2 medium onions into thin rings. Heat 2 table-spoons butter and 1 tablespoon oil in heavy-based frying pan. Add onions, cook over low heat 10–12 minutes or until onions are dark golden, stirring occasionally. Serve hot, drizzled with a little balsamic vinegar.

BAKED ONIONS

Peel 8 small onions, leaving bases intact. Place in baking dish. Brush liberally with combined 2 tablespoons melted butter and 1 tablespoon oil. Bake in moderate 350°F oven for 30 minutes or until golden brown. Serve hot.

QUICK ONION SALSA

Peel and finely slice 1 large red onion. Combine in a bowl with 2 tablespoons lime juice, 1 tablespoon olive oil, 1 teaspoon brown sugar, 1 tablespoon chopped fresh cilantro, 1 chopped tomato, and 1 finely chopped jalapeño chili. Mix well. Season to taste. Cover and set aside at room temperature 10 minutes before serving.

THYME AND ONIONS

Peel and cut 2 medium onions into eight wedges. Heat 1 table-spoon butter and 2 tablespoons oil in heavy-based frying pan. Add onions, cook over medium heat 5 minutes or until tender and golden. Stir in 1 teaspoon each chopped fresh thyme and rosemary. Cook 1 minute more. Drizzle with vinegar. Serve hot.

Cauliflower

CAULIFLOWER WITH BACON

Cut 12 oz cauliflower into small florets. Steam or microwave until just tender. Heat 1 teaspoon oil in a medium pan. Add 2 slices finely shredded bacon, cook until browned. Add cauliflower and 2 finely chopped scallions, stir to combine. Serve hot.

CAULIFLOWER CHEESE

Cut 12 oz cauliflower into medium florets. Steam until just tender. Heat 2 tablespoons butter in medium pan. Add 1 tablespoon flour and cook, stirring, 1 minute. Gradually add 3/4 cup milk. Stir until sauce boils and thickens. Take off heat and stir in 1/3 cup grated cheddar cheese until melted. Pour over cauliflower. Serve hot.

SPICED CAULIFLOWER

CAULIFLOWER AU GRATIN

CAULIFLOWER WITH BACON

CAULIFLOWER CHEESE

SPICED CAULIFLOWER

Cut 12 oz cauliflower into small florets. Heat 2 tablespoons butter and 1 tablespoon oil in wok or frying pan. Add 1/2 teaspoon each of ground turmeric, coriander, cumin and cinnamon. Cook 1 minute. Stir in 1 teaspoon brown sugar and cauliflower. Cook over medium heat until just tender. Serve hot with a dollop of yogurt or sour cream.

CAULIFLOWER AU GRATIN

Cut 12 oz cauliflower into medium florets. Steam or microwave until just tender. Heat 2 tablespoons butter in medium pan. Add 2 teaspoons flour and cook, stirring 1 minute. Gradually add 1/2 cup milk. Stir until sauce boils and thickens. Season with salt, white pepper and nutmeg. Pour over cauliflower in an ovenproof dish. Sprinkle with 1/3 cup grated cheese combined with 2 tablespoons bread crumbs. Cook under hot broiler 2 minutes until golden. Serve hot.

CAULIFLOWER WITH TOMATO SAUCE

Cut 12 oz cauliflower into medium florets. Steam or microwave cauliflower until just tender. Heat 1 tablespoon oil in medium pan. Add $1/2$ teaspoon cracked pepper, 1 teaspoon mixed Italian herbs and 1 clove crushed garlic. Cook 1 minute. Add one $14^1/2$ oz can diced tomatoes. Bring to a boil, reduce heat, simmer 5 minutes or until reduced slightly. Pour sauce over and serve hot.

PARMESAN CAULIFLOWER

Cut 12 oz cauliflower into small florets. Toss in combined $1/4$ cup all-purpose flour, 2 tablespoons finely grated Parmesan cheese and 1 teaspoon dried mixed herbs. Heat 2 tablespoons oil and 3 tablespoons butter in heavy-based frying pan. Gently cook cauliflower in batches until just tender. Drain on paper towel. Serve hot.

HOT CHILI CAULIFLOWER

Cut 12 oz cauliflower into small florets. Steam or microwave until just tender. Combine 3 tablespoons melted butter, 1 tablespoon tomato paste, 2 tablespoons chopped fresh cilantro and $1/4$ teaspoon chili powder (or to taste) in large bowl. Toss through cauliflower. Serve hot.

CAULIFLOWER WITH LIME BUTTER

Cut 12 oz cauliflower into medium florets. Steam or microwave cauliflower until just tender. Combine $1/4$ cup softened butter, 1 tablespoon lime juice, 1 teaspoon finely grated lime rind, 1 clove crushed garlic and 1 teaspoon brown sugar. Mix well. Toss through cauliflower. Serve hot.

CAULIFLOWER WITH TOMATO SAUCE

HOT CHILI CAULIFLOWER

PARMESAN CAULIFLOWER

CAULIFLOWER WITH LIME BUTTER

CREAMED PEAS

MINTED PEAS

SAUTEED PEAS AND SCALLIONS

SWEET CILANTRO PEAS

Peas

MINTED PEAS

Steam, microwave or lightly boil 2 cups frozen green peas. Toss with 1 tablespoon finely chopped fresh mint and 1/4 teaspoon brown sugar. Serve hot.

CREAMED PEAS

Steam, microwave or lightly boil 2 cups frozen green peas. Drain. Mash with a fork. Add 1 tablespoon butter and salt and freshly ground black pepper. Stir to combine. Serve hot.

SAUTEED PEAS AND SCALLIONS

Heat 2 tablespoons butter in frying pan. Add 2 cups frozen green peas, 1 clove crushed garlic and 2 finely sliced scallions. Stir over medium heat 2–3 minutes or until just tender. Serve hot.

SWEET CILANTRO PEAS

Heat 2 tablespoons butter in medium pan. Add 1 1/2 teaspoons lemon juice, 1/2 teaspoon sugar and 2 cups frozen green peas. Cook over medium heat 2–3 minutes or until just tender. Toss with 2 tablespoons finely chopped fresh cilantro leaves. Serve hot.

PEAS AND BACON

PEAS AND BACON

Heat 2 teaspoons oil in a heavy-based frying pan. Add 2 slices finely chopped bacon. Cook 1–2 minutes. Add 2 cups frozen green peas, cook over medium heat 2–3 minutes or until tender, stirring occasionally. Toss with 1 tablespoon chopped chives and 1 tablespoon chopped lemon thyme. Serve hot.

PEAS WITH BASIL AND TOMATO

Heat 2 teaspoons oil in heavy-based frying pan. Add 1 clove crushed garlic and 1/2 cup chopped canned tomatoes in juice. Cook for 1 minute. Add 2 cups frozen green peas and 1–2 tablespoons finely shredded basil. Cook for 2–3 minutes or until just tender. Serve hot.

PEAS WITH BASIL AND TOMATO

PEPPERED PEAS AND GARLIC

Heat 1 tablespoon oil in heavy-based frying pan. Add 2 cloves crushed garlic and 1 teaspoon cracked black pepper. Stir in 2 cups frozen green peas and 1/2 teaspoon sugar. Cook over medium heat 2–3 minutes or until tender. Drizzle with balsamic vinegar if desired. Serve hot.

GOLDEN ONIONS AND PEAS

Heat 1 tablespoon oil and 2 tablespoons butter in heavy-based frying pan. Add 1 medium onion, peeled and finely sliced. Cook over low heat 5 minutes or until onions are golden brown. Add 2 cups frozen green peas. Cook 2–3 minutes or until just tender. Serve hot.

PEPPERED PEAS AND GARLIC

GOLDEN ONIONS AND PEAS

SOUPS & STARTERS

SALAD BASKETS WITH BERRY DRESSING

Preparation time: 20 minutes
Total cooking time: 15 minutes
Serves 4

12 sheets phyllo pastry
1/4 cup butter, melted
6 oz salad mix (mesclun)
8 cherry tomatoes, halved
1/2 small red pepper, thinly
   sliced
1 baby cucumber, thinly sliced
1 cup blueberries, extra

Blueberry Dressing
1/2 cup olive oil
2 tablespoons balsamic
   vinegar
1 tablespoon brown sugar
1/3 cup frozen blueberries,
   thawed, lightly crushed

➤ PREHEAT OVEN to moderate 350°F. Brush the outer base of four 3 inch round 1/2-cup capacity ramekin dishes with melted butter or oil. Line two baking pans with baking paper.

1 Place one sheet of phyllo pastry on work surface. Brush pastry lightly with melted butter, place another sheet on top. Repeat with a third layer. Fold pastry in half. Using a plate as a guide, cut a 91/2 inch circle out of the pastry with a sharp knife. Place pastry over base of prepared ramekins. Carefully fold pastry around the ramekin to form a basket shape. Place on prepared pans. Repeat process for three more baskets. Bake 15 minutes or until golden. Carefully remove phyllo basket from ramekin while hot; place baskets on wire rack to cool.

2 To make Blueberry Dressing: Combine oil, vinegar and brown sugar in small bowl, add crushed berries. Mix well.

3 Combine salad mix, tomatoes, pepper, cucumber and dressing in bowl. Mix well. Spoon into pastry baskets, top with extra blueberries.

COOK'S FILE

Storage time: Phyllo baskets can be prepared up to two hours in advance. Fill with salad mixture just before serving. Dressing can be prepared one day in advance. Store in an airtight container in refrigerator.

Hint: Salad mix (mesclun) is available from most grocers. It includes a wide variety of baby lettuce leaves and edible flowers.

ROAST SWEET POTATO WITH CILANTRO PESTO AND SPRING SALAD

Preparation time: 30 minutes
Total cooking time: 30–35 minutes
Serves 6

12 oz orange sweet potato,
    peeled
2 tablespoons lemon juice
1 bunch asparagus
1 medium red pepper
1 small baby cucumber
5 oz salad mix (mesclun)

Cilantro Pesto
3¹/₃ oz pine nuts
1 red chili, seeded
2 cloves garlic
¹/₂ bunch cilantro leaves and
    stems, roughly chopped
2 teaspoons lime juice
2 tablespoons oil

➤ PREHEAT OVEN to moderate 350°F.

1 Peel sweet potato and cut into ¹/₂ inch slices. Place in a bowl, cover with ice water and lemon juice. Leave 5 minutes, drain and pat dry with paper towel.

2 Heat oil in a deep baking dish on top of stove. Add potato, lightly coat with oil. Transfer dish to oven. Bake 30 minutes or until golden. Remove; keep warm.

3 To make Cilantro Pesto: Place pine nuts in small pan. Stir over medium heat until golden. Remove from heat, cool slightly. Place pine nuts, chili, garlic, cilantro, juice and oil in a food processor bowl. Using the pulse action, process for 30 seconds or until smooth. If mixture is too thick, add a little extra oil to thin. Cover, set aside.

4 Plunge asparagus into a medium pan of boiling water. Cook for 1 minute or until just tender, drain. Plunge into bowl of ice water, drain. Pat dry with paper towel. Cut asparagus into 2 inch pieces. Cut pepper into quarters. Remove seeds and membrane. Place skin-side up on a broiler rack. Brush with oil. Broil 5 inches from heat for 5 minutes or until skin is black. Cover with damp dish towel until cool. Peel off skin. Cut pepper into long thin strips. Cut cucumber into matchstick thin strips.

Arrange salad mix, asparagus, pepper and cucumber in a serving bowl. Serve roast sweet potato separately, topped with Cilantro Pesto.

COOK'S FILE

Storage time: Except for roast pepper, which can be made one day ahead, cook and assemble this dish just before serving.

Variation: Instead of fresh peppers, roasted peppers can be bought in jars.

HOT AVOCADO SALAD

Preparation time: 20 minutes
Total cooking time: 15 minutes
Serves 6

3 medium avocados
1 medium tomato
4 slices bacon, optional
1 medium red onion, finely chopped
1 medium red pepper, finely chopped
1 stalk celery, finely chopped
2 teaspoons sugar
2 teaspoons sweet chili sauce
2 tablespoons balsamic vinegar
1 cup grated cheddar cheese

➤ PREHEAT OVEN to moderate 350°F. Brush a 10 inch pie plate with melted butter or oil.

1 Cut avocados in half lengthwise and remove pits. Scoop out two-thirds of flesh, roughly chop. Retain shells.

2 Peel, seed and finely chop tomato. Trim bacon and place on a cold broiler rack. Broil 5–6 inches from heat until crisp. Let cool slightly and chop finely. Combine avocado, tomato, bacon, onion, pepper and celery in a medium bowl. Combine sugar, chili sauce and vinegar in a small screwtop jar and shake well. Pour over ingredients in bowl and mix well.

3 Spoon filling into avocado halves, sprinkle with cheese. Place in prepared dish. Bake 7–10 minutes or until heated through. Serve immediately with corn chips, crackers or thin slices of white toast.

COOK'S FILE

Storage time: Cook this dish just before serving.

Variation: This appetizer can also be served as a Chilled Avocado Salad. Add two tablespoons of olive oil to the dressing. Replace the cheddar cheese with shavings of fresh Parmesan cheese, cover filled avocados with plastic wrap and refrigerate until chilled before serving. Do not bake.

Note: Balsamic vinegar is a flavorful, aged wine vinegar from Modena, Italy. It is available from supermarkets and specialty food stores.

1

2

3

SWEET POTATO SOUP

Preparation time: 20 minutes
Total cooking time: 1 hour
Serves 8

2 lb orange sweet potato
2 large onions
1/4 cup butter
1 clove garlic, crushed
1 tablespoon ground cumin
8 cups chicken stock
1 1/4 cups crunchy peanut butter
1 tablespoon chili sauce
salt to taste

1/4 cup chopped peanuts
1/4 cup chopped chives

➤ PEEL SWEET potato. Peel and chop onions.
1 Chop potato into 2 inch cubes. Heat butter in a deep heavy-based pan. Add onions, cook over medium-high heat 10 minutes or until golden brown.
2 Add garlic and cumin, stir-fry for 30 seconds. Add sweet potato, stir until well coated with butter. Cover, reduce heat, cook 10 minutes. Shake pan occasionally to prevent sticking. Add chicken stock, bring to boil, reduce heat, simmer 10 minutes.

3 Stir in the peanut butter and chili sauce. Simmer gently, uncovered, for 30 minutes, stirring occasionally. Add salt to taste. Serve immediately, sprinkled with chopped peanuts and chives.

COOK'S FILE

Storage time: This soup can be prepared up to three days in advance. Store, covered in refrigerator.
Hint: Spread sliced French bread with butter creamed with curry powder to taste. Bake on a baking sheet in moderate 350°F oven until golden brown. Serve hot with soup.

1

2

3

SPINACH AND SALMON TERRINE

Preparation time: 35 minutes
Total cooking time: 10 minutes
Serves 8

2 x 9 oz packages frozen
   chopped spinach
2 tablespoons butter
1/2 cup chopped scallions
1 tablespoon chopped
   fresh dill
nutmeg and pepper to taste
6 eggs
1 tablespoon cornstarch
1 tablespoon lime juice
1/4 cup grated Parmesan
   cheese

Filling
1/4 cup chopped scallions
1 teaspoon chopped fresh dill
1 tablespoon lime juice
1 tablespoon horseradish
8 oz Neufchatel cheese
6 1/2 oz sliced smoked salmon

➤ PREHEAT OVEN to moderate 350°F. Brush a shallow 12 x 10 inch baking pan with melted butter or oil. Line base and sides with baking paper, extending 2 inches extra at ends.
1 Thaw spinach and squeeze out excess moisture. Heat butter in medium pan. Add onions and dill, stir over medium heat 1 minute. Add spinach, heat through. Season with nutmeg and pepper. Remove from heat.
2 Beat eggs in medium bowl. Blend cornstarch and juice in small bowl until smooth. Combine with eggs and spinach mixture. Pour into prepared pan. Bake 7 minutes or until firm to touch. Turn onto a damp dish cloth covered with sheet of baking paper and sprinkled with cheese. Cover with a cloth and leave to cool.
3 To make Filling: Place scallions, dill, juice, horseradish and cheese in food processor bowl. Using pulse action, process 30 seconds or until smooth.
4 Cut spinach base into three strips (3 x 13 inches). Place one strip on board. Spread with filling, top with a third of smoked salmon slices.

Spread second strip with a thin layer of filling. Place cheese-side down on salmon. Repeat procedure with next layer. Decorate with rolled smoked salmon slices. Cut terrine into 3/4 inch slices to serve. Serve cool, with light salad.

COOK'S FILE

Storage time: Make this dish one day in advance. Refrigerate to let the flavor develop. Do not freeze.

GRILLED TOMATOES WITH BRUSCHETTA

Preparation time: 15 minutes
Total cooking time: 20 minutes
Serves 4

1 loaf Italian bread
4 large ripe tomatoes
1/2 teaspoon dried marjoram
  leaves
salt and freshly ground black
  pepper, to taste
2 tablespoons olive oil
2 tablespoons red wine vinegar
1 teaspoon brown sugar

2 tablespoons olive oil,
  extra
1 clove garlic, cut in half
1/2 cup chopped marinated
  artichoke hearts, undrained
1 tablespoon finely chopped
  flat-leaf parsley

➤ CUT BREAD in thick slices. Preheat broiler.

1 Cut tomatoes in half; gently squeeze out seeds. Place tomatoes cut-side up in shallow ovenproof dish. Place marjoram, salt and pepper, oil, vinegar and sugar in a small screw-top jar and shake well. Pour dressing over tomatoes.

2 Broil tomatoes 5–6 inches from heat for 10–15 minutes; turn halfway during cooking. Remove from heat; keep warm.

3 Brush bread liberally with oil on both sides; toast until golden. Rub cut surface of garlic over bread. Place cooked tomatoes onto bread, top with artichoke hearts and sprinkle with parsley. Serve immediately.

COOK'S FILE

Storage time: Cook this dish just before serving.

Note: Bruschetta are toasted Italian bread slices (or any kind of crusty bread) flavored with olive oil and garlic.

1

2

3

CORN AND CHEESE CHOWDER

Preparation time: 15 minutes
Total cooking time: 30 minutes
Serves 8

1/3 cup butter
2 large onions, finely chopped
1 clove garlic, crushed
2 teaspoons cumin seeds
4 cups chicken stock
2 medium potatoes, peeled and
  chopped
1 cup canned creamed corn
2 cups fresh corn kernels

1/4 cup chopped fresh parsley
1 cup grated cheddar cheese
salt and freshly ground black
  pepper to taste
1/4 cup cream, optional
2 tablespoons chopped fresh
  chives to garnish

➤ HEAT BUTTER in large heavy-based pan. Add onion, cook over medium-high heat 5 minutes or until golden.

1 Add garlic and cumin seeds, and cook 1 minute, stirring constantly. Add chicken stock. Bring to boil. Add potato, reduce heat. Simmer, uncovered, 10 minutes.

2 Add creamed corn, corn kernels and parsley. Bring to boil, reduce heat and simmer for 10 minutes more.

3 Stir in cheese, salt and pepper to taste and cream. Heat gently until cheese melts. Serve immediately, sprinkled with chopped chives.

COOK'S FILE

Storage time: Cook this dish up to one day in advance. Reheat and add cheese just before serving.

Variation: Corn kernels scraped from fresh young corn on the cob are best for this recipe, but frozen or canned corn may be substituted if fresh is unavailable.

1

2

3

*Grilled Tomatoes with Bruschetta (top) and
Corn and Cheese Chowder.*

EGGPLANT AND ZUCCHINI POTS WITH PEPPER RELISH

Preparation time: 12 minutes
+ 20 minutes standing
Total cooking time: 40 minutes
Makes 6

1 large eggplant, cut into
    1/2 inch cubes
1 tablespoon salt
6 1/2 oz fresh ricotta cheese
1 1/4 cups sour cream
3 eggs
1 tablespoon cornstarch
1 cup grated zucchini
1/2 teaspoon cracked black
    pepper

Pepper Relish
3/4 cup balsamic vinegar
1/3 cup sugar
1 teaspoon yellow mustard seeds
1 green apple, peeled and chopped
1 pear, peeled and chopped
1 red pepper, chopped
1 green pepper, chopped

► PREHEAT OVEN to moderately hot 375°F. Brush six 1/2 or 3/4-cup capacity ramekins with oil. Place eggplant in colander, sprinkle with salt; leave 20 minutes. Rinse under cold water; drain well.

1 Using electric beaters, beat ricotta and cream in small mixing bowl until light and creamy. Add eggs and cornstarch, beat until smooth. Transfer to large mixing bowl and gently fold in eggplant, zucchini and black pepper.

2 Spoon mixture evenly into prepared pots. Arrange in a deep baking dish. Fill dish two-thirds up side of pots with warm water; cover loosely with foil. Bake 40 minutes or until a skewer comes out clean when inserted in center. When ready to serve, top or accompany with Pepper Relish.

3 To make Pepper Relish: Heat vinegar, sugar and seeds in a medium pan 5 minutes or until sugar dissolves and mixture boils. Add remaining ingredients. Bring to boil, reduce heat and simmer, uncovered, 30 minutes.

COOK'S FILE

Storage time: Cook this dish up to one hour before serving. Relish can be made up to two days in advance.

1

2

3

TWO-CHEESE RISOTTO CAKES

Preparation time: 30 minutes + 1 hour
  15 minutes refrigeration
Total cooking time: 30 minutes
Serves 6

3¼ cups chicken stock
1 tablespoon olive oil
2 tablespoons butter
1 small onion, finely chopped
1¼ cups short-grain rice
⅓ cup freshly grated Parmesan
  cheese
1 oz mozzarella cheese, cut into
  ½ inch cubes
1¼ oz sundried tomatoes,
  chopped
oil for deep frying
3 oz mixed salad (mesclun)

➤ BOIL STOCK in small pan. Reduce heat, cover; keep gently simmering.

1 Heat oil and butter in a medium heavy-based pan. Add onion, stir over medium heat 3 minutes until golden; add rice. Reduce heat to low, stir 3 minutes or until lightly golden. Add a quarter of the stock to pan. Stir 5 minutes or until all the liquid is absorbed.

2 Repeat process until all stock has been added and rice is almost tender, stirring constantly. Stir in Parmesan. Remove from heat. Transfer to a bowl to cool; refrigerate 1 hour.

3 With wetted hands, roll two tablespoonfuls of rice mixture into a ball. Make an indentation in the ball, and press in a cube of mozzarella and a couple of pieces of sundried tomato. Reshape ball to cover completely, then flatten slightly to a disc shape. Refrigerate for 15 minutes.

4 Heat oil in a medium heavy-based pan. Gently lower risotto cakes a few at a time into moderately hot oil. Cook 1–2 minutes or until golden brown. Remove with a slotted spoon; drain on paper towels. To serve, arrange salad leaves on each plate and place three risotto cakes on top. Serve immediately.

COOK'S FILE

Storage time: Two-Cheese Risotto Cakes can be prepared up to 24 hours in advance. Store in refrigerator. Fry just before serving.

CHILI PUFFS WITH CURRIED VEGETABLES

Preparation time: 20 minutes
Total cooking time: 1 hour 5 minutes
Makes 12

1/3 cup butter
1 1/4 cups water
1 1/4 cups all-purpose flour, sifted
1/4 teaspoon chili powder
4 eggs, lightly beaten
4 yellow summer squash
4 oz snow peas
1 carrot
1/4 cup butter, extra
2 medium onions, sliced
2 tablespoons mild curry paste
10 oz small oyster mushrooms
1 tablespoon lemon juice

➤ PREHEAT OVEN to hot 425°F. Brush two baking sheets with melted butter or oil and line with baking paper. Combine butter and water in medium pan. Stir over low heat for 5 minutes or until butter has melted and mixture reaches the boil. Remove from heat; add flour and chili all at once, stir with a wooden spoon until just combined.

1 Return pan to heat, beat constantly over low heat 3 minutes or until mixture thickens and comes away from side and base of pan. Transfer mixture to large mixing bowl. Using electric beaters, beat mixture on high speed 1 minute. Add eggs gradually, beating until mixture is glossy. (This stage could take up to 5 minutes.)

2 Place two heaped tablespoons of mixture at a time onto prepared baking sheets about 4 inches apart. Bake on top shelf of preheated oven 20 minutes. Reduce heat to moderately hot 375°F and bake 30 minutes more or until crisp and well browned. (Cut a small slit into each puff halfway during cooking to allow excess steam to escape and puff to dry out.) Transfer puffs to wire rack to cool.

3 Slice squash thinly. Cut snow peas in half diagonally. Cut carrot into thin strips. Heat butter in medium pan, add onion. Cook over low heat 5 minutes or until golden; stir in curry paste. Add mushrooms and prepared vegetables, stir over high heat for 1 minute. Add lemon juice, remove from heat, stir. Cut puffs in half (see Note) and fill with vegetables. Serve immediately.

COOK'S FILE

Storage time: Cook this dish just before serving. Unfilled puffs can be frozen for up to three months.

Note: A small amount of uncooked dough mixture in the center of cooked curry puffs is a result of the large size of the puffs. Remove mixture using a spoon, then dry out the shells in a warm oven.

1

2

3

CREAMED FENNEL SOUP

Preparation time: 10 minutes
Total cooking time: 35 minutes
Serves 4

2 medium potatoes
1 medium fennel bulb
1/4 cup butter
2 cups chicken stock
salt and freshly ground black
    pepper to taste

4 oz cream cheese, chopped
1 tablespoon chopped fresh
    chives
1 tablespoon lemon juice

➤ CHOP potatoes.
1 Slice and chop fennel. Heat butter in a medium pan; add fennel. Cook, covered, over low heat for 10 minutes, stirring occasionally. Do not allow fennel to brown. Add potatoes and stock to pan, stir. Bring to boil, reduce heat to low. Cover and cook 10 minutes or until vegetables are tender. Season to taste. Remove from heat; cool slightly.
2 Transfer mixture to a food processor bowl; add cheese. Process until mixture is smooth and creamy.
3 Return soup to pan. Add chives and juice, stir over low heat until just heated through.

COOK'S FILE

Storage time: Soup can be made one day in advance. Store in refrigerator.

GREEN PEA SOUP

Preparation time: 20 minutes + 2 hours
  soaking
Total cooking time: 1 hour 40 minutes
Serves 4–6

1½ cups green or yellow
  split peas (or combination)
2 tablespoons oil
1 medium onion, finely chopped
1 stalk celery, finely sliced
1 medium carrot, finely sliced
1 tablespoon ground cumin
1 tablespoon ground coriander
2 teaspoons grated fresh ginger

5 cups chicken stock
2 cups frozen green peas
salt and freshly ground black
  pepper to taste
1 tablespoon chopped fresh mint
⅓ cup plain yogurt or sour
  cream, to serve

➤ RINSE SPLIT peas in colander under cold water.

1 Drain peas well. Heat oil in a large heavy-based pan, add onion, celery and carrot. Cook over medium heat for 3 minutes, stirring occasionally, until soft but not browned. Stir in cumin, coriander and ginger, cook 1 minute.

2 Add split peas and chicken stock to pan. Bring to a boil; reduce heat to low. Simmer, covered, for 1½ hours, stirring occasionally.

3 Add frozen peas to pan and stir to combine; set aside to cool. When cool, puree soup in batches in a blender or food processor until smooth. Return to pan; gently reheat. Season to taste. Stir in mint. Serve with a swirl of yogurt or sour cream in each bowl.

COOK'S FILE

Storage time: Soup may be made up to one day in advance and refrigerated. Reheat; stir in mint before serving.
Hint: If soup becomes too thick after refrigeration, thin with extra stock.

1

2

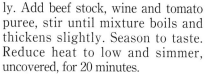
3

RICH RED ONION SOUP

Preparation time: 20 minutes
Total cooking time: 50 minutes
Serves 6

1 tablespoon oil
2 tablespoons butter
2 lb red onions
1 tablespoon all-purpose flour
4 cups beef stock
1 cup red wine
1 cup tomato puree
salt and freshly ground black
  pepper to taste

12 slices French baguette, cut
  diagonally ¾ inch thick
½ cup finely grated cheddar
  cheese

➤ HEAT OIL and butter in a large heavy-based pan.

1 Slice onions thinly. Add onions, stir-fry over a high heat for 3 minutes until soft and starting to become golden. Reduce heat to medium-low, and cook onions a further 25 minutes, stirring occasionally, until very soft and golden brown.

2 Sprinkle flour over onions, stir well with a wooden spoon to combine. Cook for 2 minutes, stirring constantly. Add beef stock, wine and tomato puree, stir until mixture boils and thickens slightly. Season to taste. Reduce heat to low and simmer, uncovered, for 20 minutes.

3 Toast baguette on both sides under a broiler. Top with grated cheese, return to broiler and cook until melted and golden. Ladle soup into deep bowls and float bread slices on top.

COOK'S FILE

Storage time: Rich Red Onion Soup may be made up to one day in advance. Store in refrigerator. Reheat soup gently, toast bread and broil cheese just before serving.

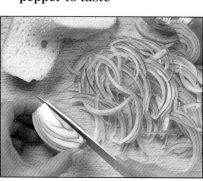
1

2

3

*Green Pea Soup (top)
and Rich Red Onion Soup.*

MUSHROOM CAPS WITH GARLIC AND THYME

Preparation time: 20 minutes
Total cooking time: 25 minutes
Serves 6

6 large flat or field mushrooms
    (about 2¹/₂ oz each)
2 tablespoons oil
1 small onion, finely
    chopped
3 slices bacon, finely chopped
2 cloves garlic, crushed
4 slices white bread

1 tablespoon fresh thyme leaves
freshly ground black pepper to
    taste

► PREHEAT OVEN to moderate 350°F. Line a large baking pan with foil, brush with oil or melted butter.

1 Using fingers, peel skin from mushrooms. Remove stems and chop finely. Heat oil in a heavy-based frying pan. Add onion and bacon and cook over medium heat until golden. Add chopped mushroom stems and garlic, cook 3 minutes over medium heat until soft, stirring occasionally.

2 Transfer to a medium mixing bowl to cool. Remove crusts from bread, tear into pieces and place in food processor bowl. Using pulse action, process 20 seconds until fluffy crumbs form.

3 Add bread crumbs and thyme to bowl and stir until well combined. Place mushrooms on prepared pan, top with bread crumb mixture. Grind pepper over. Bake for 20 minutes or until mushrooms are tender and crumbs golden. Serve immediately.

COOK'S FILE

Storage time: Topping may be prepared up to four hours in advance. Cook mushrooms just before serving.

1

2

3

INDIVIDUAL SPINACH SOUFFLES

Preparation time: 20 minutes
Total cooking time: 25 minutes
Serves 4

1/3 cup dry bread crumbs
3 oz spinach leaves
3 tablespoons butter
2 tablespoons all-purpose flour
1 cup milk
4 eggs, separated
1/2 cup finely grated cheddar
   cheese
2 tablespoons freshly grated
   Parmesan cheese
pinch cayenne pepper to taste
salt to taste
1 tablespoon freshly grated
   Parmesan cheese, extra

➤ PREHEAT OVEN to moderate 350°F. Brush four 3/4-cup soufflé dishes with melted butter or oil. Coat base and sides evenly with bread crumbs, shake off excess.

1 Wash spinach leaves thoroughly. Shred finely, and steam for 1 minute, until just tender; cool. Using your hands, squeeze all excess moisture from spinach. Spread out to separate strands, and set aside.

2 Heat butter in a medium pan; add flour. Stir over a low heat 2 minutes or until lightly golden. Add milk gradually to pan, stirring until mixture is smooth. Stir constantly over medium heat 2 minutes until mixture boils and thickens; boil 1 minute more. Remove from heat. Add egg yolks, beat until smooth. Add cheeses, cayenne and salt, stir until melted and almost smooth; stir in spinach.

3 Using electric beaters, beat egg whites in a medium, clean dry mixing bowl until stiff peaks form. Using a metal spoon, fold gently into spinach mixture.

4 Spoon into prepared dishes, bake 20 minutes or until well risen and browned. Sprinkle with extra Parmesan and serve immediately.

COOK'S FILE

Storage time: Cook soufflés just before serving. Spinach base can be prepared up to one day ahead; fold whites into mixture just before cooking.

1

2

3

4

VEGETABLE TEMPURA

Preparation time: 30 minutes + 1 hour
refrigeration
Total cooking time: 5 minutes per batch
Serves 6

1¼ cups all-purpose flour
1 egg
1¼ cups water
4 oz broccoli
1 small onion
1 small red pepper
1 small green pepper
1 medium carrot
2 oz green beans
light vegetable oil for deep
frying

Dipping Sauce
⅓ **cup soy sauce**
2 **tablespoons Thai sweet chili**
sauce
1 **clove garlic, crushed**
1 **tablespoon honey**

➤ PLACE FLOUR into large mixing bowl.

1 Make a well in the center, add egg and water and whisk until combined. Cover and refrigerate 1 hour.

2 Cut broccoli into small florets. Finely slice onion. Cut peppers and carrot into thin strips about 2½ inches long. Cut beans to about 2½ inches long, and halve lengthwise. Add vegetables to batter; stir to combine.

3 Heat oil in a medium pan. Using tongs, gather a small bunch of batter-coated vegetables (roughly two pieces of each vegetable) and lower into oil. Hold submerged in oil a few seconds until batter begins to set and vegetables hold together. Release from tongs and cook until crisp and golden. Drain on paper towels. Repeat until all vegetables are cooked. Serve immediately with dipping sauce.

To make Dipping Sauce: Place all ingredients in a small bowl and gently whisk together with a fork until combined.

COOK'S FILE

Storage time: Vegetables may be prepared up to four hours in advance. Batter and cook just before serving.

1

2

3

GRILLED EGGPLANT AND ASPARAGUS SANDWICH

Preparation time: 45 minutes
  + 30 minutes standing
Total cooking time: 40 minutes
Serves 6

2 medium eggplant
1 tablespoon olive oil
1 bunch asparagus
1/4 cup butter
1/3 cup finely chopped scallions
1/2 cup all-purpose flour
1 cup milk
1/4 cup grated romano cheese
3 1/3 oz prosciutto, finely
    shredded
1 tablespoon lemon juice
salt and freshly ground black
    pepper to taste
1 egg yolk

Soufflé Topping
1 egg white
1/4 cup grated romano cheese

➤ LINE a shallow baking pan with foil. Brush with melted butter or oil. Cut eggplant into six slices lengthwise. Sprinkle with salt, stand 30 minutes. Rinse under cold water, drain. Pat dry with paper towel.

1 Place eggplant on cold broiler rack. Brush with oil. Broil 5 inches from heat for 5 minutes or until golden brown each side. Drain on paper towel. Trim woody ends from asparagus. Steam or microwave until just tender. Cut six asparagus into 2 inch lengths, set aside. Finely chop remaining asparagus. Heat butter in medium pan. Add onions, cook over medium-high heat 1 minute. Stir in flour. Add milk gradually to pan, stirring until mixture is smooth. Stir constantly over medium heat 5 minutes or until mixture boils and thickens; boil 1 minute more.

2 Add cheese, prosciutto, juice, pepper, yolk and chopped asparagus. Mix well. Remove from heat. Place six eggplant slices on prepared pan. Spread asparagus filling evenly over each eggplant slice. Top with remaining eggplant slices.

3 To make Soufflé Topping: Preheat oven to moderate 350°F. Using electric beaters, beat egg white in small, clean mixing bowl until stiff peaks form. Spread egg whites evenly over eggplant. Sprinkle with extra cheese and decorate with the remaining asparagus. Bake for 15 minutes or until cheese is melted. Serve the sandwiches immediately.

COOK'S FILE

Storage time: This recipe can be assembled up to eight hours ahead. Prepare Soufflé Topping just before cooking.
Hint: Romano cheese and prosciutto (also known as Parma ham) are available from supermarkets or meat shops.

1

2

3

RED PEPPER SOUP

Preparation time: 20 minutes
Total cooking time: 50 minutes
Serves 6

4 medium red peppers
4 medium tomatoes
1/4 cup oil
1/2 teaspoon dried marjoram
1/2 teaspoon dried mixed herbs
2 cloves garlic, crushed
1 teaspoon mild curry paste
1 medium red onion, sliced
1 medium leek, sliced (white
    part only)
8 oz green cabbage, chopped

4 cups water
1 teaspoon sweet chili sauce
salt and freshly ground black
    pepper to taste

➤ CUT PEPPERS in quarters. remove seeds and membrane.

1 Place skin-side up on broiler rack. Brush with oil. Broil 5 inches from heat for 5 minutes or until skin is black. Cover with a damp dish towel until cool. Peel off skin. Mark a small cross on the top of each tomato. Place in a bowl of boiling water for 1–2 minutes and then immediately into cold water. Peel skin off downwards from the cross. Cut tomatoes in half and gently squeeze out seeds.

2 Heat oil in a large pan. Add herbs, garlic and curry paste. Stir over low heat for 1 minute, or until aromatic. Add onion and leek and cook 3 minutes or until pale gold. Add cabbage, tomatoes, peppers and water. Bring to boil, reduce heat and simmer 20 minutes. Remove from heat. Cool slightly.

3 Place soup in small batches in a food processor bowl. Using pulse action, process 30 seconds or until smooth. Return soup to clean pan, stir through chili sauce, season to taste. Reheat gently. Serve hot.

COOK'S FILE

Storage time: Can be made up to five days in advance and refrigerated.

ARTICHOKES WITH TARRAGON MAYONNAISE

Preparation time: 30 minutes
Total cooking time: 30 minutes
Serves 4

4 medium globe artichokes
1/4 cup lemon juice

Tarragon Mayonnaise
1 egg yolk
1 tablespoon tarragon vinegar
1/2 teaspoon Dijon mustard
2/3 cup olive oil
salt and white pepper to taste

➤ TRIM STALKS from base of artichokes.

1 Using scissors, trim points from outer leaves. Using a sharp knife, cut top from artichoke. Brush all cut areas of artichokes with lemon juice to prevent discoloration.

2 Steam artichokes for 30 minutes, until tender. Add more boiling water if necessary. Remove from heat and set aside to cool.

3 To make Tarragon Mayonnaise: Place egg yolk, vinegar and mustard in a medium mixing bowl. Using a wire whisk, beat for 1 minute. At first, add oil a teaspoon at a time, whisking constantly until mixture is thick and creamy. As the mayonnaise thickens, pour oil in a thin, steady stream. Continue whisking until all the oil is added. Season to taste. Place a cooled artichoke on each plate with a little Tarragon Mayonnaise.

COOK'S FILE

Storage time: Artichokes may be cooked up to four hours in advance. Mayonnaise may be made up to two hours in advance and refrigerated.
Hint: To eat artichokes, take off a leaf at a time, dip base of leaf in mayonnaise and scrape off fleshy base with teeth. Towards the center of the artichoke, the leaves are more tender and more of the leaf is edible. Provide a bowl for discarded leaves.

1

2

3

MAIN COURSES

MEXICAN-STYLE VEGETABLES

Preparation time: 30 minutes + 2 hours refrigeration
Total cooking time: 50 minutes
Serves 6

Polenta
1¹/3 cups chicken stock
1 cup water
1 cup yellow cornmeal
¹/2 cup freshly grated Parmesan cheese
2 tablespoons olive oil

1 large green pepper
1 large red pepper
3 medium tomatoes
6 green patty pan squash
1 ear fresh corn
1 tablespoon oil
1 medium onion, sliced
1 tablespoon ground cumin
¹/2 teaspoon chili powder
2 tablespoons chopped fresh cilantro
salt, freshly ground black pepper

➤ BRUSH an 8 inch round springform pan with oil.

1 To make Polenta: Place chicken stock and water in a medium pan and bring to a boil. Add cornmeal and stir to combine; stir constantly for 10 minutes until very thick (see Note). Remove from heat and stir in Parmesan. Spread mixture into prepared pan; smooth surface. Refrigerate 2 hours. Turn out, cut into six wedges. Brush one side with oil, broil 5 inches from heat for 5 minutes or until edges are browned. Repeat with other side.

2 Cut peppers into ³/4 inch squares, chop tomatoes, cut squash into quarters and cut corn into ³/4 inch slices, quartered.

3 Heat oil in large pan. Cook onion over medium heat 5 minutes or until soft. Stir in cumin and chili powder, cook 1 minute. Add vegetables. Bring to boil, reduce heat. Simmer, covered, over low heat 30 minutes or until vegetables are tender, stirring occasionally. Stir in cilantro, season to taste and serve hot with wedges of polenta.

COOK'S FILE

Storage time: Vegetables can be cooked up to one day in advance. Polenta can be cooked one day in advance. Broil just before serving.
Note: Polenta must be stirred for the time given, otherwise it will be gritty.

FETTUCCINE WITH CREAMY MUSHROOM AND BEAN SAUCE

Preparation time: 15 minutes
Total cooking time: 20 minutes
Serves 4

3 oz pine nuts
12 oz fettuccine
8 oz green beans
2 tablespoons oil
1 onion, chopped
2 cloves garlic, crushed
8 oz mushrooms, thinly sliced
1/2 cup white wine
11/4 cups cream
1/2 cup vegetable stock

1 egg
1/4 cup freshly chopped basil
salt and freshly ground black
   pepper to taste
1/4 cup sundried tomatoes, cut
   into thin strips
2 oz Parmesan cheese, shaved

➤ PLACE PINE NUTS in small pan. Stir over medium heat until golden. Set aside. Cook fettuccine in a large pot of boiling water with a little oil added until just tender. Drain and keep warm.

1 Trim tops and tails of beans and cut into long thin strips.

2 Heat oil in a large heavy-based frying pan. Add onion and garlic, cook over medium heat 3 minutes or until softened. Add mushrooms, cook, stirring, for 1 minute. Add wine, cream and stock. Bring to a boil, reduce heat, simmer for 10 minutes.

3 Lightly beat egg in a small bowl. Stirring constantly, add a little cooking liquid to the egg. When combined, pour mixture slowly into pan, stirring constantly for 30 seconds. Add beans, basil, pine nuts and sundried tomatoes, stir until heated through. Season to taste. To serve, divide pasta between warmed serving plates, pour sauce over. Garnish with Parmesan. Serve immediately.

COOK'S FILE

Storage time: Cook this dish just before serving.

1

2

3

VEGETABLE LASAGNA

Preparation time: 20 minutes
Total cooking time: 1 hour 15 minutes
Serves 6

3 large red peppers
2 large eggplant
2 tablespoons oil
1 large onion, finely chopped
3 cloves garlic, crushed
1 teaspoon dried mixed herbs
1 teaspoon dried oregano
1 lb mushrooms, sliced
16 oz can whole tomatoes, crushed
15 oz can red kidney beans, drained
1 tablespoon sweet chili sauce
8 oz package no-cook lasagna
salt and freshly ground black pepper to taste
1 bunch spinach, chopped
1 cup basil leaves
$3^{1}/_{3}$ oz sundried tomatoes, sliced
$1/4$ cup grated Parmesan cheese
$1/4$ cup grated cheddar cheese

Cheese Sauce
$1/4$ cup butter
$1/4$ cup all-purpose flour
2 cups milk
$1^{1}/_{4}$ lb ricotta cheese

▶ PREHEAT OVEN to moderate 350°F. Brush a 13 x 9 inch 10–15 cup capacity) ovenproof casserole dish with melted butter or oil.

1 Cut peppers in quarters. Remove seeds and membrane. Place skin-side up on broiler rack. Brush with oil. Broil 10 minutes or until skin is black. Cover with damp dish towel until cool. Peel off skin. Cut peppers into long thin strips. Set aside. Slice eggplant into $1/2$ inch rounds. Place eggplant in large pan of boiling water. Cook 1 minute or until just tender, drain. Pat dry with paper towel. Set aside.

2 Heat oil in a large heavy-based frying pan. Add onion, garlic and herbs. Cook over medium heat 5 minutes or until onion is soft. Add mushrooms, cook 1 minute. Add tomatoes, beans, sauce, salt and pepper. Bring to boil, reduce heat. Simmer, uncovered, 15 minutes or until sauce thickens. Remove from heat. Dip lasagna sheets in hot water to soften slightly and arrange four sheets in prepared dish.

3 Arrange half of each of the eggplant, spinach, basil, pepper, mushrooms mixture and sundried tomatoes over pasta. Top with a layer of pasta; press gently. Repeat layers. Top with cheese sauce, sprinkle with combined Parmesan and cheddar cheeses. Bake

for 45 minutes or until pasta is soft.

4 To make Cheese Sauce: Heat butter in medium pan, add flour. Stir over medium heat 2 minutes or until mixture is golden. Add milk gradually, stirring until mixture boils and thickens. Boil 1 minute. Add ricotta, stir until smooth.

COOK'S FILE

Storage time: This dish can be frozen, uncooked, for up to one month.

VEGETABLE STIR-FRY

Preparation time: 15 minutes
Total cooking time: 5 minutes
Serves 4

2 scallions
8 oz broccoli
1 medium red pepper
1 medium yellow pepper
5 oz button mushrooms
1 tablespoon oil
1 teaspoon sesame oil
1 clove garlic, crushed

2 teaspoons grated ginger
1/4 cup halved pitted black olives
1 tablespoon soy sauce
1 tablespoon honey
1 tablespoon sweet chili sauce
1 tablespoon sesame seeds

➤ FINELY SLICE scallions. Cut broccoli in small florets.

1 Cut peppers in halves, remove seeds and membrane. Cut into thin strips. Cut mushrooms in half.

2 Heat oils in a wok or large frying pan. Add garlic, ginger and scallions. Stir-fry over medium heat 1 minute.

Add broccoli, peppers, mushrooms and olives. Stir-fry for further 2 minutes or until vegetables are bright in color and just tender.

3 Combine soy sauce, honey and chili sauce in a bowl. Mix well. Place sesame seeds in a baking pan, toast in a moderate 350°F oven until golden. Pour sauce over vegetables, toss lightly to combine. Sprinkle with sesame seeds and serve immediately.

C O O K ' S   F I L E

Storage time: Cook this dish just before serving.

1

2

3

SQUASH GNOCCHI WITH SAGE BUTTER

Preparation time: 30 minutes + 5 minutes standing
Total cooking time: 1 hour 45 minutes
Serves 4

1 lb winter squash
1 1/2 cups all-purpose flour
1/4 cup freshly grated Parmesan cheese
freshly ground black pepper

Sage Butter
1/3 cup butter
2 tablespoons chopped fresh sage

1/4 cup freshly grated Parmesan cheese, extra

➤ PREHEAT OVEN to moderate 350°F. Brush a baking pan with oil or melted butter.

1 Cut squash into large pieces and place on prepared pan. Bake 1 1/2 hours, until very tender. Cool slightly. Scrape flesh from skin, avoiding any tough or crispy parts. Place into a large mixing bowl. Sift flour into bowl, add Parmesan cheese and pepper. Mix until well combined. Turn onto a lightly floured surface, knead 2 minutes or until smooth.

2 Divide dough in half. Using floured hands, roll each half into a sausage about 16 inches long. Cut into 16 equal

pieces. Form each piece into an oval shape, indent with floured fork prongs.

3 Heat a large pan of water until boiling. Gently lower batches of gnocchi into water. Cook until gnocchi rise to the surface, and then 3 minutes more. Drain and keep warm.

To make Sage Butter: Melt butter in small pan, remove from heat and stir in sage. Set aside for 5 minutes to keep warm.

To serve, divide gnocchi between bowls, drizzle with Sage Butter and sprinkle with extra Parmesan cheese.

C O O K ' S   F I L E

Storage time: Gnocchi can be prepared up to four hours in advance. Cook just before serving.

1

2

3

Vegetable Stir-fry (top)
and Squash Gnocchi with Sage Butter.

POTATO CAKES WITH SHRIMP AND ZUCCHINI

Preparation time: 20 minutes
Total cooking time: 30 minutes
Serves 6

3 medium zucchini
2 cups finely grated potato
1 egg, lightly beaten
1 teaspoon ground paprika
1/2 cup all-purpose flour
1/4 cup oil
1/4 cup butter
1/2 bunch chives, chopped
1 tablespoon chopped fresh dill
1/2 cup all-purpose flour, extra
2 cups milk

1/4 cup chopped parsley
salt and freshly ground black
　　pepper to taste
1 tablespoon lime juice
1 lb small shrimp, peeled

➤ CUT ZUCCHINI into 2 inch slices.
1 Drain potato. Pat dry with paper towel. Combine potato, egg and paprika in mixing bowl. Shape quarter cups of mixture into balls. Roll in flour and flatten slightly. Heat oil in frying pan. Cook potato cakes in batches over medium heat 2–3 minutes each side or until golden. Drain on paper towel.
2 Heat butter in medium pan. Add chives and zucchini. Cook over medium heat 5 minutes or until tender. Remove, drain on paper towels. Add

dill and extra flour to pan. Stir over low heat 2 minutes or until flour mixture is lightly golden.
3 Add milk gradually to pan, stirring until smooth. Stir constantly over medium heat 4 minutes or until mixture boils and thickens. Boil for further 1 minute. Add parsley, salt, pepper and lime juice. Stir in shrimp and zucchini. Heat gently. Pour over potato cakes. Serve hot.

COOK'S FILE

Storage time: Shrimp/zucchini mixture can be prepared a day in advance. Store in refrigerator, reheat gently.
Variation: Omit shrimp or replace with another sliced green vegetable. Cook with the chives and zucchini.

1

2

3

CARROT PESTO SLICES

Preparation time: 45 minutes
Total cooking time: 50 minutes + 30
minutes standing
Serves 4

3 tablespoons butter
1/2 cup all-purpose flour
3 cups milk
2/3 cup light sour cream
1 teaspoon cracked black
   pepper
3 oz cheddar cheese, grated
4 eggs, lightly beaten
2 tablespoons bottled pesto
1 1/2 lb carrots, peeled and grated
8 oz package no-cook lasagna

2 oz cheddar cheese, grated,
   extra

➤ BRUSH an 11 x 7 inch ovenproof baking dish with melted butter or oil.
1 Heat butter in large pan; add flour. Stir over low heat until mixture is lightly golden and bubbling. Add combined milk, sour cream and pepper gradually to pan, stirring until mixture is smooth. Stir constantly over medium heat 5 minutes or until mixture boils and thickens; boil further 1 minute, remove from heat. Stir in cheese, cool slightly. Add beaten eggs gradually, stirring constantly, mix well.
2 Pour one-third of sauce into another bowl for topping; set aside. Add pesto

and carrot to remaining sauce, stirring to combine.
3 Preheat oven to slow 300°F. Beginning with layer of carrot mixture, alternate layers of carrot with lasagna sheets in prepared dish. Use three layers of each, finishing with pasta. Spread reserved sauce evenly over the top. Sprinkle with extra cheese. Leave for 15 minutes before cooking (to allow pasta to soften). Bake 40 minutes or until set and firm to touch. Remove from oven, cover and set aside 15 minutes prior to serving (this ensures dish will slice cleanly).

COOK'S FILE

Storage time: Cook this dish just before serving.

PEPPER FRITTATA

Preparation time: 15 minutes
Total cooking time: 40 minutes
Serves 4

5 x 4 oz jars pimento pieces
4 slices bacon, optional
1 tablespoon olive oil
2 medium red onions, finely
    chopped
6 eggs, lightly beaten
1/2 cup grated cheddar cheese
1/2 cup Parmesan cheese
1 tablespoon all-purpose flour

1/4 cup chopped fresh parsley
salt to taste
1/2 teaspoon cracked black
    pepper

➤ PREHEAT OVEN to moderate 350°F. Brush a 9 inch oven proof pie plate with melted butter or oil.
1 Rinse pimento pieces, drain. Pat dry with paper towel. Cut into thin strips. Trim fat from bacon and place bacon on cold broiler rack. Broil 5 inches from heat or until crisp. Drain on paper towel. Cut into small pieces.
2 Heat oil in medium pan. Add onions, cook over medium heat 2 minutes.

Remove and drain on paper towels.
3 Combine eggs, pimento, bacon and onions in a large bowl. Add combined cheese and flour, parsley and salt and pepper. Mix well. Spoon into prepared pie plate. Bake 25–30 minutes or until set and firm to touch. Serve hot or cold with a green salad and crusty bread.

COOK'S FILE

Storage time: Cook this dish just before serving.
Hint: Pimento is bottled red pepper. Substitute two fresh red peppers, roasted, peeled and chopped if desired.

1

2

3

VEGETABLE PIE

Preparation time: 40 minutes + 30 minutes standing
Total cooking time: 50 minutes
Serves 6

1 small eggplant
2 tablespoons butter
2 cloves garlic, crushed
2 scallions, sliced
6$^{1}/_{2}$ oz orange sweet potato, peeled, cut into $^{1}/_{2}$ inch cubes
1 medium carrot, thinly sliced
2 oz button mushrooms, sliced
1 small red pepper, finely sliced
5 oz broccoli, cut in small florets
3 tablespoons butter, extra
2 tablespoons all-purpose flour
1$^{1}/_{2}$ cups milk
4 oz feta cheese, crumbled
$^{1}/_{4}$ cup grated Parmesan cheese
2 tablespoons pine nuts, toasted
1 teaspoon dried oregano
2 eggs, lightly beaten
2 frozen puff pastry sheets, thawed
1 egg, extra, lightly beaten

➤ BRUSH a 9 inch round pie plate with melted butter or oil.

1 Cut eggplant into 1 inch cubes. Place in a colander, sprinkle with salt. Leave for 30 minutes. Rinse under cold water, drain. Pat dry with paper towel. Preheat oven to moderate 350°F.

2 Heat butter in large pan. Add garlic and scallions, cook over medium heat 1 minute. Add sweet potato, carrot and mushrooms. Cook, stirring, 4 minutes or until vegetables are just tender. Add pepper and broccoli. Cook further 3 minutes. Add eggplant, cook 2 minutes more. Remove from heat.

3 Melt extra butter in medium pan. Add flour, stir over medium heat 1 minute or until mixture is lightly golden and bubbling. Add milk gradually to pan, stirring until mixture is smooth. Stir constantly over medium heat 4 minutes or until mixture boils and thickens. Add feta, Parmesan, pine nuts and oregano. Combine vegetable mixture and sauce in a large bowl. Add eggs, stir until well combined. Spoon into prepared dish.

4 Cut a long strip of pastry just wider than rim of the pie plate. Brush rim of the plate with water and press down strip. Brush strip with water. Roll remaining pastry sheet to $^{1}/_{8}$ inch thickness. Place pastry over top, press edges to seal. Trim and decorate edge. Cut out shapes from pastry top to allow steam to escape and use the cut-outs to decorate the pie top. Brush top with egg. Bake for 35–40 minutes or until golden brown and puffed.

COOK'S FILE

Storage time: This pie is best eaten on the day it is made.

GOURMET VEGETABLE PIZZA

Preparation time: 30 minutes
+ 30 minutes standing
Total cooking time: 1 hour 10 minutes
Serves 6

Pizza Dough
1/3 cup fresh basil leaves
2 tablespoons cornmeal
1 envelope active dry
   yeast
1 teaspoon sugar
1 1/2 cups all-purpose flour
1/2 cup warm water
1 teaspoon salt
1 tablespoon olive oil

Tomato Sauce
1 tablespoon oil
1 small red onion, finely
   chopped
1 clove garlic, crushed
1 large tomato, finely
   chopped
1 tablespoon tomato paste
1/2 teaspoon dried oregano

Topping
2 oz button mushrooms, finely
   sliced
4 oz canned baby corn
1 1/2 cups grated mozzarella
   cheese
2 oz spinach leaves, finely
   shredded
1 small red pepper, cut into
   short thin strips
2 tablespoons pine nuts

➤ FINELY CHOP basil leaves.
1 Brush a 12 inch pizza pan with oil and sprinkle with cornmeal.
2 To make Pizza Dough: Combine yeast, sugar and 2 tablespoons of the flour in a small mixing bowl.

Gradually add water; blend until smooth. Set aside, covered with plastic wrap, in a warm place for about 10 minutes or until foamy.
3 Place remaining flour into a large mixing bowl. Add salt and basil, make a well in the center. Add yeast mixture and oil. Using a knife, mix to a soft dough.
4 Turn dough onto a lightly floured surface, knead for 5 minutes or until smooth. Shape dough into a ball, place in a large, lightly oiled mixing bowl. Leave, covered with plastic wrap, in a warm place for 20 minutes or until well-risen. While dough is rising, prepare sauce.
5 To make Tomato Sauce: Heat oil in a small pan, add onion and garlic and cook over a medium heat for 3 minutes or until soft. Add tomato, reduce heat and simmer for 10 minutes, stirring occasionally. Stir in tomato paste and oregano, cook for a further 3 minutes. Allow sauce to cool before using.
6 Preheat oven to hot 425°F. Turn dough out onto a lightly floured surface, knead a further 5 minutes until smooth. Roll out to fit prepared pan. Spread sauce onto pizza base, arrange mushrooms and corn evenly on top. Sprinkle over half the cheese, top with spinach, pepper and remaining cheese. Sprinkle with pine nuts. Bake for 40 minutes or until crust is golden. Serve pizza immediately.

COOK'S FILE

Storage time: Tomato Sauce may be made up to four hours in advance. Pizza is best prepared and cooked just before serving.
Hint: Look for canned baby corn with other canned corn products. Alternatively, you may like to use fresh corn scraped off the cob as a substitute.

1

2

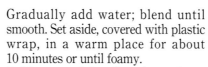

3

4

5

6

SWEET SPICED BABY PUMPKINS

Preparation time: 35 minutes
Total cooking time: 1 hour
Serves 4

4 golden nugget pumpkins
1 tablespoon olive oil
1 cup brown and wild rice blend
10 oz orange sweet potato
2 tablespoons butter
1 medium onion, finely chopped
1 cup chopped scallions
2 teaspoons ground cumin
1/2 teaspoon ground ginger
1 teaspoon ground coriander
1 teaspoon ground turmeric

1 teaspoon garam masala
2 tablespoons raisins, soaked in
    hot water
1/3 cup grated cheese

➤ PREHEAT OVEN to moderate 350°F. Slice the top third off each pumpkin horizontally.

1 Scoop out seeds, leaving a deep cavity. Brush lightly with oil. Stand pumpkins in baking dish. Pour in enough water to come halfway up the sides of the pumpkins. Place lid on each. Bake 20 minutes. Remove from water bath, allow to cool. Cook rice in large pan of boiling water until tender. Drain and cool.

2 Peel sweet potato and cut into 1/2 inch cubes. Heat butter in frying pan. Add onion and sweet potato. Cover and cook over medium heat 5 minutes. Add scallions and cook, uncovered, 1 minute. Stir in spices, cook 2 minutes. Remove from heat. Fold in rice and drained raisins.

3 Spoon filling into pumpkin cavities. Sprinkle with cheese. Place lid on at an angle. Cover with foil. Place in a baking dish. Return to oven for 20 minutes. Serve hot with salad.

COOK'S FILE

Storage time: Cook this dish just before serving.

Note: Brown and wild rice mix is available in pre-packaged mixes from supermarkets. If unavailable, white or brown rice can be used.

1

2

3

VEGETABLE TART

Preparation time: 30 minutes + 20 min-
utes refrigeration
Total cooking time: 1 hour
Serves 6

1¼ cups all-purpose flour
⅓ cup butter, chopped
2–3 tablespoons ice water

Vegetable Filling
1 small red pepper
1 small green pepper
6½ oz winter squash
1 medium potato
5 oz broccoli
1 medium carrot
1 tablespoon oil
1 medium onion, finely sliced
3 tablespoons butter
¼ cup all-purpose flour
1 cup milk
2 egg yolks
½ cup grated cheddar cheese
½ cup grated cheddar cheese,
extra

➤ PREHEAT OVEN to moderate 350°F. Sift flour into large bowl; add butter. Using fingertips, rub butter into flour for 2 minutes until mixture is fine and crumbly. Add almost all water, mix to firm dough, adding more water if necessary. Turn onto lightly floured surface, press together until smooth. Roll out and line a deep 9 inch fluted tart pan. Refrigerate 20 minutes. Cut a sheet of wax paper large enough to cover pastry-lined pan. Spread a layer of dried beans evenly over paper. Bake 10 minutes, remove from oven, discard paper and beans. Return to oven for 10 minutes or until lightly golden. Cool.
1 To make Vegetable Filling: Cut pepper, squash and potato into ¾ inch squares. Cut broccoli into

florets. Cut carrots into ⅝ inch slices.
2 Heat oil in a frying pan, add onion and cook over medium heat 5 minutes, until soft and golden. Add pepper and cook, stirring, 5 minutes until soft. Transfer to a large mixing bowl to cool. Steam or boil remaining vegetables for 3 minutes, until just tender. Drain well, add to bowl and cool.
3 Heat butter in a small pan; add flour. Stir over a low heat 2 minutes or until flour mixture is lightly golden. Add milk gradually to pan, stirring until

mixture is smooth. Stir constantly over medium heat until mixture boils and thickens; boil 1 minute more, remove from heat. Add yolks, beat until smooth. Stir in cheese. Pour sauce over cooked vegetables, and stir to thoroughly combine. Pour mixture into pastry shell, sprinkle with extra cheese. Bake for 25 minutes, until top is golden.

COOK'S FILE

Storage time: Cook this dish just before serving.

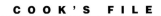

1

2

3

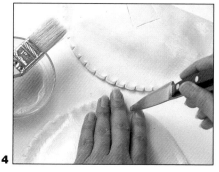

4

BRAISED CABBAGE TURNOVERS

Preparation time: 15 minutes
Total cooking time: 1 hour 5 minutes
Makes 6

1¼ lb green cabbage
¼ cup butter
2 onions, thinly sliced
1 stalk celery, thinly sliced
¼ cup water
6 scallions, finely
    chopped
¼ cup chopped parsley
¼ teaspoon ground chili
    powder
3 oz feta cheese, crumbled
salt and freshly ground black
    pepper to taste
6 frozen puff pastry sheets,
    thawed
1 egg, lightly beaten

➤ PREHEAT OVEN to hot 425°F.
Line two large baking sheets with
baking paper.

1 Finely shred cabbage. Heat butter
in medium pan; add onions and celery.
Cook over low heat 15 minutes, stirring occasionally. Add cabbage and
water. Stir over high heat 10 minutes
or until cabbage has wilted and
almost all liquid has evaporated.

2 Add scallions, parsley and chili to
pan; stir. Remove pan from heat; cool
mixture slightly. Add cheese, mix
well; season to taste, cool.

3 Roll pastry sheets out until ⅛ inch
thick. Brush each sheet with egg.
Divide cabbage mixture evenly into six
portions. Place one portion of mixture
at a time slightly off-center on pastry
square. Fold sheet in half, press to seal
edges. Cut pastry into a half circle
using a 7 inch saucepan lid as a guide;
discard excess pastry. Repeat process
with remaining pastry and filling.

4 Brush tops of half circles with
remaining egg. Using a sharp knife,
cut a diamond pattern across top of
pastry. (Do not cut through the pastry.)
Use finger and back of knife to decorate
edge. Arrange pies on prepared baking
sheets; bake 40 minutes or until puffed
and browned. Serve warm or cool.

COOK'S FILE

Storage time: This dish can be
made up to one day in advance.

SWEET AND SOUR NOODLES AND VEGETABLES

Preparation time: 12 minutes
Total cooking time: 15 minutes
Serves 4–6

6½ oz thin fresh egg noodles
4 canned baby corn
¼ cup oil
1 green pepper, sliced
1 red pepper, sliced
2 stalks celery, sliced diagonally
1 carrot, sliced diagonally
8 oz button mushrooms, sliced
1 tablespoon cornstarch

2 tablespoons wine or balsamic vinegar
1 teaspoon chopped fresh chili
2 teaspoons tomato paste
2 chicken bouillon cubes, crumbled
1 teaspoon sesame oil
14½ oz can pineapple chunks or tidbits
3 scallions, sliced diagonally

➤ COOK NOODLES in large pan of boiling water for 3 minutes; drain well.

1 Slice corn diagonally. Heat oil in wok; add pepper, celery, carrot and mushrooms. Stir over high heat for 5 minutes.

2 Add corn and noodles. Reduce heat to low; cook 2 minutes. Blend cornstarch with vinegar in small mixing bowl until smooth. Add chili, tomato paste, bouillon cubes, oil and undrained pineapple, stir to combine.

3 Pour pineapple mixture over ingredients in wok. Stir over medium heat 5 minutes or until mixture boils and sauce thickens. Add scallions; serve immediately.

COOK'S FILE

Storage time: Cook this dish just before serving.

Variation: Thinly sliced Chinese barbecued pork (char su) can be added to this dish, if desired.

1

2

3

STUFFED BABY PUMPKINS

Preparation time: 15 minutes
Total cooking time: 50 minutes
Makes 4

4 medium baby pumpkins
1/4 cup water
1/2 cup cooked rice
2 teaspoons curry paste
1 tablespoon finely chopped
    fresh cilantro
1 green apple, finely chopped
1 small zucchini, finely
    chopped
1 small carrot, finely chopped

2 oz button mushrooms, thinly
    sliced
4 oz bunch asparagus spears,
    chopped
2 teaspoons raisins
1/4 teaspoon garam masala
1/4 cup butter, melted

➤ PREHEAT OVEN to hot 425°F. Cut top off each of the pumpkins and set aside. Scoop out seeds and discard.

1 Arrange pumpkins in a medium ovenproof pan; replace tops. Add water to dish and cover firmly with foil, bake 30 minutes. Remove pan from oven, remove pumpkins, drain water and brush dish with melted butter or oil.

2 Combine rice, curry paste, cilantro, apple, zucchini, carrot, mushrooms, asparagus, raisins, spice and butter in a medium bowl; mix well.

3 Spoon rice and vegetable mixture into cavity of pumpkin. Top each pumpkin with lid. Cover with foil and bake, covered, in preheated oven for 20 minutes or until vegetables are just cooked.

COOK'S FILE

Storage time: Cook this dish just before serving.
Hint: To give the filled pumpkins a shiny appearance, brush the shell and lid with melted butter or oil before serving.

CARAMELIZED ONION AND SPINACH TART

Preparation time: 25 minutes
  + 10 minutes standing
Total cooking time: 2 hours
Serves 6

1 cup all-purpose flour
1/3 cup butter, chopped
1 egg yolk
1 tablespoon water

Filling
5 medium (2 lb) onions, thinly
  sliced
3/4 cup water
1/4 cup brown sugar
2 tablespoons balsamic vinegar
1 bay leaf
3 whole dried chilies

Topping
2 cups finely chopped fresh
  spinach
1 cup grated cheddar cheese
1/4 cup all-purpose flour
1/4 teaspoon baking power
1 teaspoon mustard powder
1/8 teaspoon salt
1/4 cup cream
2 eggs, lightly beaten

➤ PREHEAT OVEN to hot 425°F. Brush an 8 inch round springform pan with melted butter or oil.

1 Place flour and butter in food processor bowl. Using the pulse action, process for 15 seconds or until mixture is fine and crumbly. Add egg yolk and water to bowl, process for 20 seconds until mixture is smooth.

2 Press pastry evenly over base of prepared pan; refrigerate 10 minutes. Cut a sheet of wax paper large enough to cover pastry-lined pan. Spread a layer of rice evenly over paper. Bake

20 minutes; remove from oven and discard rice. Set pastry aside to cool. Combine onions, water, sugar, vinegar, bay leaf and chilies in medium heavy-based pan. Stir over medium heat until sugar has dissolved and mixture is boiling. Reduce heat and simmer, covered, 1 hour, stirring occasionally. Drain any excess liquid; discard bay leaf and chilies.

3 Spread cooled onion mixture evenly

over pastry base. Spoon topping over onion. Bake 45 minutes or until topping is golden. Serve warm or cool.
To make Spinach Topping: Place all ingredients in large mixing bowl; mix well.

COOK'S FILE

Storage time: Make up to one day in advance and store in the refrigerator. Reheat gently before serving.

1

2

3

SPICY WINTER CASSEROLE

Preparation time: 35 minutes +
  overnight soaking
Total cooking time: 1 hour 15 minutes
Serves 6

1 small eggplant, cut into
  ¾ inch cubes
1 tablespoon salt
1 cup dried chickpeas (garbanzo
  beans)
2 tablespoons olive oil
2 medium onions, sliced
2 cloves garlic, crushed
2 tablespoons grated fresh
  ginger
1 tablespoon ground cumin

2 teaspoons paprika
¼ teaspoon saffron threads
1½ teaspoons chili powder
6 cups vegetable stock
2 medium carrots, thinly sliced
2 medium turnips, cut into
  ¾ inch cubes
3 medium zucchini, cut into
  ¾ inch slices
10 oz winter squash, cut into
  1¼ inch cubes
2 medium tomatoes, chopped
⅓ cup chopped flat-leaf parsley

➤ SPREAD EGGPLANT out in a single layer and sprinkle generously with salt. Stand for 20 minutes, rinse well and pat dry with paper towel.

1 Place chickpeas in a medium bowl, cover with water and soak overnight.

2 Heat oil in a large pan. Add onions and cook over a medium heat 5 minutes until golden, stirring occasionally. Add garlic, ginger and spices, stir-fry a further 1 minute. Drain chickpeas and add to pan with stock. Bring to boil, reduce heat, cover and simmer 40 minutes, until chickpeas are just tender. Stir occasionally.

3 Add carrots and turnips to pan, simmer 15 minutes. Add remaining vegetables. Simmer, covered, 15 minutes until vegetables are tender, stirring occasionally. Stir in parsley and serve with rice.

COOK'S FILE

Storage time: Casserole may be made up to two days in advance. Store in refrigerator.

HERBED POTATO BAKE

Preparation time: 12 minutes
Total cooking time: 1 hour
Serves 4–6

6 medium potatoes
2 red onions
2 large zucchini
2 scallions
3⅓ oz salami (optional)
1¼ cups sour cream
2 cloves garlic, crushed

2 tablespoons chopped fresh
  parsley
2 tablespoons chopped fresh
  chives
salt and freshly ground black
  pepper to taste
¼ cup bread crumbs

➤ PREHEAT OVEN to moderate 350°F. Brush a large, shallow ovenproof dish with melted butter.

1 Using a sharp knife, slice the potatoes, onions, zucchini, scallions and salami thinly.

2 Combine sliced vegetables and salami with cream, garlic, herbs and salt and pepper in a large bowl; mix well. Transfer mixture to prepared dish; smooth surface. Bake, covered with foil, 20 minutes. Remove foil.

3 Sprinkle bread crumbs over vegetable mixture. Bake on top shelf of oven for 40 minutes or until golden and potatoes are tender.

COOK'S FILE

Storage time: Cook this dish just before serving.

*Spicy Winter Casserole (top)
and Herbed Potato Bake.*

VEGETABLE RISOTTO

Preparation time: 15 minutes
Total cooking time: 30 minutes
Serves 6

5½ cups chicken stock
1 bunch asparagus, cut into
    1¼ inch lengths
2 medium zucchini, cut into
    ¾ inch slices
3 oz snow peas, cut into
    ¾ inch lengths
2 tablespoons olive oil
1 medium onion, finely chopped

1½ cups short-grain rice
2 small tomatoes, chopped
½ cup grated Parmesan cheese

➤ PLACE CHICKEN STOCK in a medium pan. Cover, bring to boil. Reduce heat and keep at a simmer.
1 Place asparagus, zucchini and snow peas in a medium heatproof bowl, cover with boiling water. Let stand 2 minutes, drain. Refresh with cold water, drain well.
2 Heat oil in a large heavy-based pan. Add onion, stir over medium heat until golden; add rice. Reduce heat to medium low, stir rice for 3 minutes or

until lightly golden. Add one quarter of the stock to the pan, stir constantly for 7 minutes or until stock is absorbed.
3 Repeat the process until all but half a cup of stock has been used, and rice is almost tender. Add vegetables with the remaining stock, stir for 5 minutes until liquid is absorbed and vegetables are tender. Stir in Parmesan cheese and serve risotto immediately.

COOK'S FILE

Storage time: Cook this dish just before serving.

SPINACH FETTUCCINE WITH RICH TOMATO SAUCE

Preparation time: 15 minutes
Total cooking time: 40 minutes
Serves 4

4 large ripe tomatoes
2 tablespoons olive oil
1 medium onion, finely chopped
2 cloves garlic, crushed
1 tablespoon red wine vinegar
1/4 cup tomato paste
1 teaspoon sugar

1 teaspoon dried oregano leaves
1 teaspoon dried basil leaves
1 lb spinach fettuccine

➤ MARK A SMALL CROSS on the bottom of each tomato.
1 Place tomatoes in boiling water for 1–2 minutes, then immediately into cold water. Remove from water, and peel skin down from cross. Roughly chop tomatoes.
2 Heat oil in a medium heavy-based pan. Add onion and cook over a medium heat for 5 minutes, until lightly golden, stirring occasionally. Add garlic and cook for 1 minute. Add

tomatoes and vinegar, bring to a boil. Reduce heat to medium low and simmer, uncovered, for 25 minutes; stirring occasionally.
3 Add tomato paste, sugar and herbs. Simmer 15 minutes, stirring often. Cook fettuccine in a large pan of boiling water until just tender; drain. Place on serving plates, top with tomato sauce and serve immediately.

COOK'S FILE

Storage time: Cook pasta just before serving. The tomato sauce can be frozen for up to six months.

LEEK AND TURNIP PIE

Preparation time: 45 minutes
Total cooking time: 1 hour +
   12 minutes
Makes one 10 inch pie

2 cups all-purpose flour
1/2 cup butter, chopped
1/2 cup grated Parmesan cheese
1–2 tablespoons ice water

Filling
1/3 cup butter
1 1/2 lb white turnips, washed,
   peeled and thinly sliced
2 medium leeks
2 tablespoons caraway seeds
2 tablespoons brown sugar
2 tablespoons red wine vinegar
1/4 cup chopped fresh basil
2 tablespoons all-purpose flour
salt and freshly ground black
   pepper to taste
4 oz cheddar cheese, grated
1/4 cup grated Parmesan cheese
1 egg, lightly beaten

► PREHEAT OVEN to moderate
350°F. Brush a 10 inch pie plate with
melted butter or oil.

1 Sift flour into large bowl; add butter. Using fingertips, rub butter into
flour until mixture is fine and
crumbly. Add cheese and almost all
the liquid, mix to a firm dough,
adding a little more water if necessary. Turn onto a lightly floured surface, knead 2 minutes or until smooth.
2 Divide dough in two. Roll out one
portion of pastry between two sheets
of baking paper, large enough to cover
base and sides of prepared plate. Trim
edges. Cut a sheet of wax paper large
enough to cover pastry-lined pie plate.
Spread a layer of dried beans evenly
over paper. Bake 8 minutes. Remove
from oven; discard paper and beans.
Return pastry to oven for 5 minutes or
until lightly golden. Cool.
3 Slice leeks finely. Heat butter in
large pan, add turnips and leeks. Cook
over medium heat 4 minutes or until
coated with butter. Cover, cook for
10 minutes, shaking pan occasionally
to prevent sticking. Add caraway
seeds and brown sugar. Stir until
sugar melts. Add vinegar, cook
1 minute. Remove from heat, cool
slightly. Stir in basil and 1 tablespoon
of flour. Season to taste.
4 Spoon one-third of turnip mixture
over pastry. Combine remaining flour

and cheeses. Sprinkle one-third over
turnip mixture. Continue layering, finishing with cheese. Roll remaining
pastry into 1 1/2 inch diameter log, cut
into 2 inch slices. Place overlapping
pastry circles around edge of pie.
Brush between each round with egg.
Bake 30–40 minutes or until golden.

COOK'S FILE

Storage time: Cook this dish just
before serving.

VEGETABLE PILAF

Preparation time: 20 minutes
Total cooking time: 35 minutes
Serves 4

1/4 cup olive oil
1 medium onion, sliced
2 cloves garlic, crushed
2 teaspoons ground cumin
2 teaspoons paprika
1/2 teaspoon allspice
1 1/2 cups long-grain rice
1 1/2 cups vegetable stock
3/4 cup white wine
3 medium tomatoes, chopped
5 oz button mushrooms, sliced
2 medium zucchini, sliced
5 oz broccoli, cut into florets

➤ HEAT OIL in a large heavy-based pan.

1 Add onion, cook for 10 minutes over medium heat until golden brown. Add garlic and spices, cook 1 minute until aromatic.

2 Add rice to pan, stir until well combined. Add vegetable stock, wine, tomatoes and mushrooms, bring to a boil. Reduce heat to low, cover pan with tight-fitting lid. Simmer for 15 minutes.

3 Add zucchini and broccoli to pan, replace lid and cook further 5–7 minutes, until vegetables are just tender. Serve immediately.

COOK'S FILE

Storage time: Cook this dish just before serving.

Hint: Sliced pepperoni, salami, chopped bacon or peeled shrimp may be added with onion.

SIDE DISHES

SUGAR PEAS AND CARROTS IN LIME BUTTER

Preparation time: 10 minutes
Total cooking time: 10 minutes
Serves 4

4 oz carrots
4 oz sugar snap peas
1/4 cup butter
2 cloves garlic, crushed
1 tablespoon lime juice
1/2 teaspoon brown sugar
1 lime

➤ PEEL CARROTS and cut into thin diagonal slices.

1 Wash and string sugar snap peas. Heat butter in a large heavy-based frying pan. Add garlic, cook over low heat for 1 minute. Add juice and sugar. Cook, stirring over heat until sugar has completely dissolved.

2 Add peas and carrots, cook over medium heat 2–3 minutes or until tender but still crisp. Serve hot. Garnish with lime zest.

3 To make lime zest: Peel lime rind into long strips using a vegetable peeler. Remove all white pith. Cut into long thin strips with a sharp knife.

COOK'S FILE

Storage time: Cook this dish just before serving.

Hints: Because of the sweet flavor, this dish is an excellent way to encourage children (who may be otherwise unenthusiastic) to eat their vegetables.

To obtain the maximum amount of juice from limes, place in microwave oven on High for 30 seconds. This will soften the fruit and allow the juice to be easily squeezed.

An easy alternative to crushing garlic yourself is to purchase ready-crushed bottled garlic.

Variations: Snow peas or green beans can be used in place of sugar snap peas. Baby carrots also make a very attractive addition to this recipe – leave a portion of the green tops on. If limes are unavailable, substitute lemon juice and zest.

This dish can also be adapted to make a lovely light salad. To make the salad, replace the butter with 2 tablespoons of olive oil and cook according to the recipe. Let cool to room temperature and serve as a side salad with meat or seafood dishes or as part of a vegetarian meal. Sprinkle with finely chopped cashews or toasted pine nuts, if desired.

SQUASH WITH CHILI AND AVOCADO

Preparation time: 20 minutes
Total cooking time: 10 minutes
Serves 6

1½ lb winter squash
2 tablespoons olive oil
1 tablespoon chopped fresh
    cilantro leaves
1 tablespoon chopped fresh mint
2 teaspoons sweet chili sauce
1 small red onion, finely
    chopped
2 teaspoons balsamic vinegar
1 teaspoon brown sugar
salt to taste
1 large avocado

➤ SCRAPE SEEDS from inside of squash.

1 Cut squash into thin slices. Remove skin. Cook in a large pan of simmering water until tender but still firm. Remove from heat; drain well.

2 Combine oil, cilantro, mint, chili, onion, vinegar and sugar in a small bowl. Mix well. Cut avocado in half. Remove pit using a sharp-bladed knife. Peel skin from avocado. Discard. Cut avocado in thin slices.

3 Combine warm pumpkin and avocado in a serving bowl. Gently toss with cilantro dressing. Serve immediately.

COOK'S FILE

Storage time: Assemble this dish just before serving. Cilantro dressing can be made up to several hours in advance. Store, covered, in the refrigerator.

Variation: Add one small red chili, finely chopped, to dressing if desired. For a milder flavor, remove the seeds and membranes of the chili.

EGGPLANT AND TOMATO CAPONATA

Preparation time: 25 minutes
Total cooking time: 15 minutes
Serves 4

1 lb small eggplant
2 tablespoons salt
1 medium onion
3 stalks celery
2 medium tomatoes
1/2 cup olive oil
1 tablespoon capers, lightly
    crushed
1 tablespoon sugar
2 tablespoons white wine vinegar
salt and freshly ground black
    pepper to taste

➤ SLICE EGGPLANT in half lengthwise. Cut in thin slices. Place on a flat tray. Sprinkle with salt and leave for 20 minutes.

1 Cut onion in thin slices. Cut celery into thin slices diagonally. Mark a small cross in the base of each tomato. Place in boiling water for 1–2 minutes and then immediately into cold water. Peel skin off downwards from the cross. Cut into wedges. Squeeze gently to remove seeds.

2 Heat 1 tablespoon of oil in a large frying pan. Add onion; cook over medium heat 2 minutes or until soft and slightly golden. Add celery, cook 2 minutes. Add tomatoes, capers, sugar, vinegar and salt and pepper to taste. Cook for 5 minutes. Remove from heat. Set aside.

3 Rinse eggplant, drain. Pat dry with paper towel. Heat remaining oil in a medium frying pan, add eggplant. Cook over medium heat for 4–5 minutes or until soft and golden brown. Drain eggplant on paper towel. Add eggplant to onion mixture. Stir until well combined. Leave to cool. Serve at room temperature.

COOK'S FILE

Storage time: This dish can be made two days in advance. Store in an airtight container in refrigerator. Bring to room temperature to serve.
Hints: Sliced green olives can be added to this dish if desired. Add them with the capers.
Caponata goes well with broiled fish such as tuna, or broiled steak.

1

2

3

TWO-POTATO HASH BROWNS

Preparation time: 20 minutes
Total cooking time: 25 minutes
Serves 4–6

3 slices bacon, finely chopped
    (optional)
8 oz orange sweet potato, peeled
1 lb potatoes, peeled
1 large onion, finely chopped
2 tablespoons olive oil
salt and freshly ground black
    pepper to taste
sour cream

2 tablespoons chopped fresh
chives

➤ PREHEAT OVEN to moderate 350°F. Brush a baking sheet with melted butter or oil. Grease an egg ring to use as mold for hash browns.
1 Place bacon in small pan. Cook over medium-high heat 3 minutes. Drain on paper towel. Chop finely. Cut potato and sweet potato in half. Cook in boiling water for 10 minutes or until just starting to cook; drain well and grate.
2 Place potatoes, onion, bacon, oil, salt and pepper in a bowl. Toss well to ensure even mixing. Press spoonfuls of mixture into egg ring on a tray.

Level surface. Remove ring and repeat with remaining mixture until all the mixture is shaped.
3 Bake 20 minutes or until crisp and golden or shallow fry in a little oil and melted butter Serve immediately, topped with sour cream and chives.

COOK'S FILE

Storage time: Raw mixture can be prepared 12 hours in advance. Store, covered, in the refrigerator.
Note: Hash browns can be pan-fried in a small amount of oil. To obtain a crisp result, it is essential that the moisture is squeezed out of the potato before mixing with other ingredients.

SCALLION AND CELERY BUNDLES

Preparation time: 20 minutes
Total cooking time: 10 minutes
Serves 6

4 stalks celery
1 bunch scallions
2 tablespoons butter
1 teaspoon celery seeds
1 tablespoon honey
1/2 cup chicken stock
1 teaspoon soy sauce
1 teaspoon cornstarch
1 teaspoon water

➤ CUT CELERY into 4 inch lengths, then into strips the same thickness as the scallions.

1 Cut root from scallions. Cut into 4 inch lengths. Reserve scallion tops for ties. Plunge scallion tops into boiling water 30 seconds or until bright green, then plunge immediately into ice water. Drain and pat dry with paper towel.

2 Combine scallion and celery stalks. Divide into six bundles. Tie each bundle firmly with a scallion top.

3 Heat butter in frying pan. Fry bundles quickly over medium-high heat, 1 minute each side. Remove from pan. Add celery seeds, cook 30 seconds.

Add honey, stock, soy sauce and blended cornstarch and water. Bring to boil, reduce heat, stirring continuously. Add scallion and celery bundles. Simmer gently 7 minutes or until bundles are just tender. Serve immediately with a little of the cooking liquid.

COOK'S FILE

Storage time: Bundles can be assembled up to 12 hours in advance. Cover with damp dish towel and store in refrigerator. Cook just before serving.
Hint: This side dish is suitable to accompany meat, fish or poultry dishes. Use beef stock in place of chicken, if preferred.

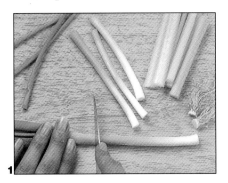

1

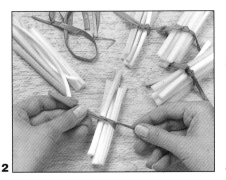

2

3

SPROUT AND PEAR SALAD WITH SESAME DRESSING

Preparation time: 30 minutes + 50 minutes refrigeration
Total cooking time: None
Serves 6

8 oz snow pea sprouts or
  watercress
8 oz fresh bean sprouts
1 bunch chives
3¹/₃ oz snow peas
1 stalk celery
2 firm pears

¹/₂ cup cilantro sprigs

Sesame Dressing
2 tablespoons soy sauce
1 teaspoon sesame oil
1 tablespoon brown sugar
2 tablespoons peanut oil
1 teaspoon rice vinegar
black or white sesame seeds

➤ WASH AND DRAIN snow pea sprouts or watercress.
1 Remove brown tip from bean sprouts. Cut chives into 1¹/₂ inch-lengths. Cut snow peas and celery into thin matchstick strips.
2 Peel and core pears. Cut into thin strips slightly wider than celery and snow peas. Cover with water to prevent discoloring.
To make Sesame Dressing: Combine all ingredients in small screwtop jar and shake well.
3 Drain pears. Combine all salad ingredients in large serving bowl. Pour in dressing, toss lightly to combine. Sprinkle with sesame seeds. Serve immediately.

COOK'S FILE

Storage time: Dressing can be prepared two days ahead. Store in refrigerator. Make salad just before serving.
Hint: Cooked shrimp may be added.

1

2

3

STIR-FRIED CHINESE VEGETABLES

Preparation time: 15 minutes
Total cooking time: 7 minutes
Serves 4

10 oz baby bok choy
3 oz green beans
3 scallions
5 oz broccoli
1 medium red pepper
2 tablespoons oil
2 cloves garlic, crushed
2 teaspoons grated ginger
1 tablespoon sesame oil
2 teaspoons soy sauce

➤ WASH AND TRIM thick stalks from bok choy.

1 Cut leaves into wide strips. Cut green beans into 2 inch lengths, and slice scallions diagonally. Cut broccoli into small florets. Cut pepper into diamonds about 3/4 inch wide.

2 Heat oil in large heavy-based frying pan or wok. Add garlic and ginger and cook over medium heat for 30 seconds, stirring constantly. Add beans, scallions and broccoli, stir-fry for 3 minutes.

3 Add pepper, stir-fry a further 2 minutes; add bok choy and stir-fry for 1 minute more. Stir in sesame oil and soy sauce, toss through. Transfer the vegetables to a serving dish and serve immediately.

COOK'S FILE

Storage time: Cook this dish just before serving.

Hint: It is important not to overcook vegetables when stir-frying. Use the minimum amount of oil and cook over medium-high heat, stirring and tossing the vegetables constantly. They will soften slightly but should never

be cooked to a limp and greasy state. Add leafy green vegetables last when stir-frying, and cook only until the leaves have just softened. Cutting vegetables into thin, even-sized pieces and on the diagonal helps them to cook quickly.

Variations: Use any Chinese vegetables in this dish. Add a little hoisin sauce at the end of cooking, if desired.
Note: Sesame oil is available at supermarkets and Chinese food stores. It is usually added at the end of cooking and used sparingly.

SAVORY FENNEL CRUMBLE

Preparation time: 20 minutes
Total cooking time: 40 minutes
Serves 6

2 fennel bulbs
1/4 cup lemon juice
2 tablespoons lemon juice, extra
salt and freshly ground black
   pepper to taste
1 tablespoon honey
1 tablespoon all-purpose flour
1 1/4 cups cream

Crumble Topping
3/4 cup rolled oats
1/2 cup all-purpose flour

1 cup rye bread crumbs, made
   from 3 slices bread
1/4 cup butter
1 clove garlic, crushed

➤ PREHEAT OVEN to moderate
350°F. Brush an 8-cup capacity ovenproof serving dish with melted butter
or oil.
1 Trim fennel and cut into thin slices.
Wash and drain well. Bring a large
pan of water to boil. Add lemon juice
and fennel slices. Cook over medium
heat 3 minutes. Drain and rinse under
cold water.
2 Place fennel in large bowl. Add
extra juice, pepper and honey and toss
to combine. Sprinkle with flour. Spoon
into prepared dish. Pour cream over
top of mixture.

3 To make Crumble Topping:
Combine oats, flour and bread
crumbs. Heat butter in small pan. Add
garlic, cook 30 seconds. Pour over
crumble ingredients and mix well.
Sprinkle mixture over fennel. Bake
20–30 minutes or until fennel is tender
and crumble is browned.

COOK'S FILE

Storage time: This dish can be
assembled up to eight hours in advance.
Store, covered, in refrigerator. Bring to
room temperature before baking.
Hints: White or wholewheat bread
crumbs can be used in place of rye
bread. Fennel has an aniseed flavor.
Blanching it before use softens the
texture slightly and reduces the
strong flavor.

ALMOND AND BROCCOLI
STIR-FRY

Preparation time: 5 minutes
Total cooking time: 5 minutes
Serves 4

1 teaspoon coriander seeds
1 lb broccoli
1/4 cup olive oil
2 tablespoons slivered
   almonds
1 clove garlic, crushed

1 teaspoon finely shredded
   ginger
2 tablespoons red wine vinegar
1 tablespoon soy sauce
2 teaspoons sesame oil
1 teaspoon toasted sesame
   seeds

➤ PUT CORIANDER SEEDS in a
plastic bag, hit with a rolling pin to
crack.
1 Cut the broccoli into small florets.
2 Heat oil in wok or large heavy-
based frying pan. Add coriander seeds

and almonds. Stir quickly over medium heat for 1 minute or until the
almonds are golden.
3 Add garlic, ginger and broccoli to
pan. Stir-fry over high heat 2 minutes.
Remove pan from heat. Pour combined vinegar, sauce and oil into wok.
Toss until broccoli is well coated.
Serve warm or cold, sprinkled with
sesame seeds.

COOK'S FILE

Storage time: This dish may be prepared two hours ahead of serving.

Savory Fennel Crumble (top)
and Almond and Broccoli Stir-fry.

MEDITERRANEAN-STYLE BRAISED LETTUCE

Preparation time: 5 minutes
Total cooking time: 3 minutes
Serves 4

12 large romaine lettuce leaves
1/3 cup olive oil
1/2 red pepper, cut into fine matchstick strips
2 scallions, cut into 1/2 inch pieces
1 tablespoon chopped fresh chives
1 tablespoon lemon juice
2 teaspoons crumbled feta cheese
1/4 teaspoon cracked black pepper

➤ TEAR EACH LETTUCE leaf into four pieces. Heat oil in medium pan; add pepper. Stir over low heat for 1 minute.

1 Add lettuce to pan, toss over high heat 1 minute or until leaves are well coated with oil. Remove lettuce from pan. Reduce heat to low.

2 Add scallions, chives and juice to pan; cook covered for 30 seconds. Remove pan from heat.

3 Combine lettuce and scallion mixture. Place on serving plate. Sprinkle with feta and black pepper. Serve warm or cold.

COOK'S FILE

Storage time: This dish can be prepared up to two hours before serving.
Note: The beauty of this dish is in the quick cooking. It is important to have all the ingredients on hand before beginning to cook, as prolonged cooking causes the lettuce to develop a bitter flavor and lose color.
Serve with barbecued fish or chicken.

BARBECUED MARINATED VEGETABLES

Preparation time: 20 minutes + 1 hour
  marinating
Total cooking time: 10 minutes
Serves 4–6

3 slender eggplant
3 medium zucchini
1 medium red pepper
1 medium green pepper
1 medium red onion
2 cloves garlic, crushed
2 teaspoons finely chopped
  fresh basil
2 teaspoons chopped fresh
  thyme leaves
1/4 cup olive oil
2 tablespoons balsamic vinegar

➤ CUT EGGPLANT and zucchini into diagonal 3/4 inch thick slices.

1 Cut pepper into 3/4 inch wide strips, and onion into eight wedges.

2 Place all vegetables into a large mixing bowl. Add the garlic, herbs, olive oil and vinegar, toss lightly to combine. Cover with plastic wrap and let stand for 1 hour.

3 Preheat grill. Drain vegetables from marinade. Place on lightly greased grill rack. Cook over medium-high heat 8–10 minutes, until tender and slightly charred, turning once. Serve with barbecued meat.

COOK'S FILE

Storage time: Vegetables may be prepared and cooked up to one hour ahead. Serve at room temperature.

1

2

3

CHILI SWEET POTATO AND EGGPLANT CHIPS

Preparation time: 5 minutes
Total cooking time: 20 minutes
Serves 4–6

1 orange sweet potato (10 oz)
1 slender eggplant (11 oz)
oil for deep frying
¼ teaspoon ground chili
    powder
¼ teaspoon ground coriander
1 teaspoon salt

➤ PEEL sweet potato.
1 Cut sweet potato and eggplant into long thin strips, similar in size. Place in a large bowl, mix.
2 Heat oil in a deep heavy-based pan. Gently lower half the combined sweet potato and eggplant into the moderately hot oil. Cook over medium-high heat for 10 minutes or until golden and crisp. Carefully remove the chips from the oil with tongs or slotted spoon. Drain on paper towels. Repeat cooking process with remaining sweet potato and eggplant.
3 Combine chili, coriander and salt in small bowl. Sprinkle all the mixture over hot chips. Toss until well coated. Serve immediately.

COOK'S FILE

Storage time: Cook this dish just before serving.
Hint: These tasty chips go well with casual dishes, such as grilled chicken breasts on rolls with salad.

ZUCCHINI WITH CUMIN CREAM

Preparation time: 5 minutes
Total cooking time: 12 minutes
Serves 4–6

1 lemon
4 large zucchini
2 tablespoons butter
1 tablespoon oil
1/2 teaspoon cumin seeds
1/2 cup cream

salt and freshly ground black
   pepper to taste

➤ GRATE RIND from lemon to make
1/2 teaspoon and squeeze 2 teaspoons
lemon juice. Set aside.
1 Cut zucchini into 2 inch thick
diagonal slices. Heat butter and oil in a
large frying pan; add half the zucchini.
Cook over medium-high heat 2 minutes
each side or until golden. Remove from
pan; drain on paper towels; keep warm.
Repeat with remaining zucchini.
2 Add seeds to pan, stir over low

heat 1 minute. Add rind and juice;
bring to boil. Add cream to pan, boil
2 minutes or until sauce thickens
slightly (see Note); season to taste.
3 Return zucchini to pan. Stir over
low heat 1 minute or until just heated
through. Serve warm or cold.

COOK'S FILE

Storage time: Cook this dish up to
one hour before serving. Refrigerate
until ready to serve.
Note: Do not boil sauce for too long
as it may separate.

POTATO AND POPPY SEED FOCACCIA

Preparation time: 30 minutes + 1 hour rising
Total cooking time: 40 minutes
Serves 4

2 cups all-purpose flour
1 envelope active dry yeast
1 teaspoon sugar
1 teaspoon salt
1¹/3 cups mashed potato
¹/4 cup warm water
¹/3 cup olive oil
2 tablespoons semolina
1 egg, lightly beaten
salt and white pepper to taste
2 teaspoons poppy seeds

➤ SIFT FLOUR into large mixing bowl.

1 Add yeast, sugar, salt and mashed potato. Pour in combined water and oil. Using a knife or spatula, mix to a soft dough.

2 Turn dough onto a well-floured surface, knead for 10 minutes, until smooth. Sprinkle surface with more flour as necessary. Shape into a ball, place into a large, lightly oiled mixing bowl. Leave, covered with plastic wrap, in a warm place for 30 minutes, until well risen.

3 Preheat oven to moderate 350°F. Knead dough again for 5 minutes. Sprinkle the base of a greased 9 inch square cake pan with semolina. Press dough into pan with floured hands. With a skewer, prick four rows of four holes into dough. Cover with plastic wrap and leave in a warm place for a further 20 minutes, until well-risen. Brush lightly with the beaten egg and sprinkle with poppy-seeds. Bake 40 minutes, until golden brown. Turn focaccia onto a wire rack to cool.

COOK'S FILE

Storage time: Focaccia is best served on the day it is made; however, it is also delicious split and toasted when one or two days old.

Hint: This recipe is open to many variations in flavor. Fresh or dried herbs may be kneaded into the dough. Try sprinkling sesame seeds or sliced olives instead of poppy seeds. The potato adds moisture to the dough.

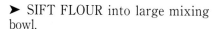

ASPARAGUS AND SNOW PEA SALAD

Preparation time: 15 minutes
Total cooking time: 5 minutes
Serves 4–6

6¹/2 oz snow peas
1 bunch asparagus spears

Dressing
2 tablespoons peanut oil
1 tablespoon sesame oil
1 tablespoon rice vinegar or red wine vinegar
¹/2 teaspoon sugar
1 tablespoon sesame seeds

➤ TOP AND TAIL snow peas.

1 Trim any woody ends from asparagus. Cut spears diagonally in half. Place in a pan of boiling water. Cook for 1 minute, then drain and plunge into ice water. Drain well.

2 **To make Dressing:** Place oils, vinegar and sugar in a small screwtop jar and shake well. Place asparagus and snow peas in a serving bowl. Pour dressing over; toss to combine.

3 Place sesame seeds in a dry frying pan. Cook over a medium heat for 1–2 minutes until lightly golden, sprinkle over salad. Serve immediately.

COOK'S FILE

Storage time: Vegetables may be prepared up to four hours in advance; dressing may be added up to one hour in advance.

Hint: Rice vinegar is available at supermarkets and Chinese food stores.

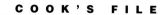

Potato and Poppyseed Focaccia (top)
and Asparagus and Snow Pea Salad.

WARM TOMATO AND HERB SALAD

Preparation time: 20 minutes
Total cooking time: 15 minutes
Serves 6

1 clove garlic, crushed
1 tablespoon olive oil
12 slices French bread, cut
    ³/4 inch thick
1 tablespoon olive oil, extra
8 oz cherry tomatoes
8 oz yellow pear tomatoes
¹/4 cup shredded basil
    leaves

1 tablespoon chopped fresh
    tarragon
¹/4 cup chopped fresh parsley
salt and freshly ground black
    pepper to taste

➤ PREHEAT OVEN to moderate 350°F.

1 Place garlic and oil in a small bowl and stir to combine. Brush one side of bread lightly with oil, place on a baking sheet. Bake for 7 minutes. Turn bread over, brush other side and bake a further 5 minutes. Set aside to cool.

2 Heat oil in a frying pan. Add whole tomatoes and stir-fry over a medium heat for 2 minutes, until just soft.

3 Add herbs to tomatoes, stir-fry for 1 minute further until well combined. Serve warm with croûtons.

COOK'S FILE

Storage time: Croûtons can be made up to eight hours in advance, cooled completely and stored in an airtight container. Tomatoes should be cooked just before serving.

Hint: Yellow pear tomatoes are similar in size to cherry tomatoes. If unavailable, use all cherry tomatoes. Miniature tomatoes are easy to grow. They are more insect-resistant than large tomatoes and can even be grown in a pot on a sunny balcony.

1

2

3

HONEYED BABY TURNIPS WITH LEMON THYME

Preparation time: 10 minutes
Total cooking time: 7 minutes
Serves 4

1 lb baby turnips
3 tablespoons butter
1/4 cup honey
1 tablespoon lemon juice

1/2 teaspoon grated lemon rind
1 tablespoon chopped fresh
  lemon thyme leaves

➤ RINSE AND lightly scrub turnips under water.
1 Trim tips and stalks. Cook in pan of boiling water 1 minute. Drain, refresh under cold water, drain well.
2 Heat butter in a medium pan; add honey. Bring mixture to boil, add lemon juice and rind. Boil over high heat for 3 minutes. Add turnips to honey and lemon mixture in pan. Cook over high heat for 3 minutes or until the turnips are almost tender and well glazed. (Test turnips with a skewer.)
3 Add lemon thyme. Remove pan from heat. Toss until turnips are well coated. Serve warm.

COOK'S FILE

Storage time: Cook this dish up to one hour before serving.
Variation: Baby carrots or baby beets can be used in this recipe.

SPICED BAKED BEETS

Preparation time: 15 minutes
Total cooking time: 1 hour 25 minutes
Serves 6

12 small beets (1 1/2 lbs)
2 tablespoons olive oil
1 teaspoon ground cumin
1 teaspoon ground coriander
1/2 teaspoon ground cardamom
1/2 teaspoon nutmeg
1 tablespoon sugar
1 tablespoon red wine vinegar

➤ PREHEAT OVEN to moderate 350°F. Brush a shallow baking pan with melted butter or oil.

1 Trim leafy tops from beets and wash thoroughly. Place in prepared pan and bake for 1 hour 15 minutes, until very tender. Set aside to cool slightly. Peel skins from beets. Trim tops and tails to neaten.

2 Heat oil in a large pan. Add spices and cook 1 minute, stirring constantly, over medium heat. Add sugar and red wine vinegar, stir for 2–3 minutes, until sugar dissolves.

3 Add beets to pan, reduce heat to low and stir gently for 5 minutes, until beets are well glazed. Serve warm or cold.

COOK'S FILE

Storage time: This dish can be cooked up to two days in advance. Store, covered, in refrigerator.

Hint: This dish is ideal for picnic fare. Serve Spiced Baked Beets with cold or hot roast meats or poultry.

Variation: Small potatoes, sliced sweet potatoes, peeled small onions or even Brussels sprouts can be cooked in this way. Bake until soft and glaze as in Step 3. Brussels sprouts should be lightly steamed rather than baked.

1

2

3

INDEX

USEFUL INFORMATION

All the recipes in this book have been double-tested by our team of home economists to ensure high standards of accuracy. All the cup and spoon measurements used are level. We have used large (2 oz) eggs in all of the recipes. The sizes of cans available vary from manufacturer to manufacturer and between countries—use the can size closest to the one suggested in the recipe.

Glossary of Terms

Blanch: To plunge vegetables into boiling water for about 1 minute, then plunge into ice cold water. This helps them retain their color, crispness and nutritional value.

Cracked pepper: Small pieces of cracked peppercorns made in a coarse grinder. May be bought ready ground.

Garnish: An edible trimming on the dish to add color and enhance appearance.

Matchsticks: Vegetables cut into fine sticks, often referred to as "julienne".

Peeling tomatoes: To remove the skin from a tomato: mark a small cross on the bottom. Plunge the tomato into boiling water for 1–2 minutes, then plunge it into cold water. Peel skin down from the cross.

Process: To use either a food processor or a blender to finely chop or puree ingredients.

Shred: To slice or shave in a downward motion using a large chef's knife. On firm vegetables such as carrots, use a zester for shredding.

Simmer: To heat a liquid until small bubbles form and it is on the point of boiling.

Oven Temperatures

Cooking times may vary slightly depending on the type of oven you are using. Before you preheat the oven, we suggest that you refer to the manufacturer's instructions to ensure proper temperature control.

For convection ovens check your appliance manual, but as a general rule, you will need to set the oven temperature a little lower than the temperature indicated in the recipe.

	°F
Very slow	250
Slow	300
Warm	325
Moderate	350
Mod. hot	375
Mod. hot	400
Hot	425
Very hot	450

Cup Conversions

1 cup bread crumbs, dry	= 3 1/3 oz
fresh	= 2 2/3 oz
1 cup cheese, grated	
cheddar (firmly packed)	= 4 oz
mozzarella	= 4 3/4 oz
Parmesan	= 3 1/3 oz
1 cup all-purpose flour	= 4 oz
wholewheat	= 4 3/4 oz
1 cup pasta, short (eg. macaroni)	= 5 oz
1 cup semolina	= 4 oz

This 1997 Crescent edition is published by Random House Value Publishing, Inc.,
201 East 50th Street, New York, N.Y. 10022.

Random House
New York·Toronto·London·Sydney·Auckland
http://www.randomhouse.com/

Printed and bound in the United States of America.

A CIP catalog record for this book is available from the Library of Congress
ISBN 0-517-18398-6

8 7 6 5 4 3 2 1